# HOW TO LIVE A MAXIMIZED LIFE

*How to Live a Maximized Life*
Copyright © 2021
Rodney Lewis Boyd

ISBN: 978-1-952474-65-1

Cover concept and design by David Warren.

All rights reserved. No part of this book may be reproduced, stored in a retrieval system, or transmitted in any form or by any means—electronic, mechanical, photocopy, recording or otherwise—without the prior written permission of the publisher. The only exception is brief quotations for review purposes.

Unless otherwise noted, all scripture quotations are taken from the New American Standard Bible®, Copyright © 1960, 1962, 1963, 1968, 1971, 1972, 1973, 1975, 1977, 1995 by The Lockman Foundation. Used by permission. (www.Lockman.org)

Scripture quotations marked "AMP" taken from the Amplified® Bible, Copyright © 1954, 1958, 1962, 1964, 1965, 1987 by The Lockman Foundation Used by permission. (www.Lockman.org)

Scripture quotations marked "KJV" taken from the King James Version of the Bible, public domain.

All references to "Strong's" refer to Strong's Exhaustive Concordance of the Bible, public domain.

Published by WordCrafts Press
Cody, Wyoming 82414
www.wordcrafts.net

# HOW TO LIVE A MAXIMIZED LIFE

## RODNEY LEWIS BOYD

WordCrafts Press

## DEDICATION

I want to dedicate this book to the most positive person in my life, my wife of 48+ years, Brenda. When I met her back in 1969, I was a mess, and by the time we got married I got even messier. She has stuck with me in the good, bad, and ugly times. She led me to the Lord in 1972 and was with me as I learned and walked out the principles found in this book.

I want to dedicate this book to my son Phillip, and his wife Jamie. Jamie is one of the most positive things that ever happen to my son.

I want to dedicate this book to my granddaughter, the grandest thing that happened to me, Emerson Grace. When this negative world presses in on me, when I see a picture of her or she crawls up in my lap, negativity dissipates.

I want to dedicate this book to anyone who has ever sat under my teachings or read any of my books as you watched me work out these positive things in a negative world.

Last but not least, I dedicate this book to the most positive influence in my life, Jesus the Christ, the Anointed One who was and is anointed with yoke-breaking, burden-lifting, oppression-removing, healing power of the Holy Ghost and power (duNAmis, dynamic ability). Now that is positive thinking right there.

# CONTENTS

Dedication ................................................................................iv
Introduction............................................................................... 1
Jesus Is Lord And Savior ............................................................7
The Principles Of........................................................................9
The Word About Words ...........................................................13
The Kingdom Principle............................................................21
The Prayer Principle.................................................................33
The Faith Principle ..................................................................36
The Servant Principle............................................................... 50
The Healthy Roots Principle....................................................55
The Money, Money, Money Principle .....................................62
Prelude To The Secret Principle...............................................68
The Peace Principle ..................................................................71
The Secret Principle .................................................................75
The Thinking Imagination Speaking Principle ..................... 80
The Tithe/Giving Principle......................................................87
The Formula For Life Principle .............................................101
The Living Water Principle....................................................104
The Love Principle..................................................................113
The Victory Principle..............................................................119
The Suffering Principle ..........................................................125
The Helping The Poor Principle ............................................134
The Dreams, Desires, Goals, Vision Principle .......................138

| | |
|---|---|
| The Discipline With Purpose Principle | 144 |
| The Will On Earth Principle | 149 |
| The Strength And Supply Principle | 151 |
| The Benefits Package Principle | 159 |
| The Mindset Principle | 167 |
| The Coffee Cup Theology Principle | 176 |
| The Mountain Moving Principle | 181 |
| The Good Report Principle | 186 |
| The Communication System Principle | 190 |
| The Love Principle | 194 |
| Final Thoughts…Finally | 200 |

# INTRODUCTION

As we live out our lives on planet Earth, we have a choice to live a *negative lifestyle* or live a *positive lifestyle*. Over the years some people written books about having a Positive Mental Attitude (P.M.A.). These books are about how to be successful in life, and in some people's minds the books are about how to *"get rich quick."* The idea is that if you only think positive thoughts, if you only speak positive words, you will only do positive things, and then you will have a positive life. On the surface, that really does sound like a good way to live, but without a relationship with the Lord, those positive vibes will soon turn into negative vibes.

For sure many people are hucksters, charlatans, scam artists, and flim-flam artists—some who claim to be Christians—who are out for themselves and to make a buck, who have the root of evil deep in their hearts, which is the love of money. Remember that money is *not* the root of all kinds of evil, but the *love* of *(lust for)* money is.

> *"For the love of money is a root of all sorts of evil, and some by longing for it have wandered away from the faith and pierced themselves with many griefs."*
> ~I Timothy 6:10

I wrote this book to make sure that true believers in Jesus Christ the Risen Savior do not throw out the baby with the bathwater concerning *true prosperity* and *true success*. I believe that the church has been duped into thinking that *poverty* is spiritual and that being *wealthy* is evil. There are a lot of people who have more money and stuff than I do, but I dare say that I have more peace than some of those people. At the same time I know people who are very rich and are at peace with their God and His blessings in their lives. Folks who look at people who are better off than they are with envy and jealousy risk becoming self-righteous which can lead to an attitude that they are better than their wealthy counterparts.

The problem with the get-rich-quick scam artist type of philosophy is that everything is *human-centered*.

> *I am the master of my fate. I am the captain of my soul*
> *Invictus*
> ~William Ernest Henley, 1849–1903

This sounds good, but the only mention of God in Invictus is;

> *I thank whatever gods may be, for my unconquerable soul.*

*Whatever gods?* This type of philosophy is based on making us gods. It is *humanism on steroids*.

HUMANISM: A variety of ethical theory and practice that emphasizes *reason, scientific inquiry, and human fulfillment* in the natural world and often rejects the importance of belief in God.
~Dictionary.com

The problem with this type of thinking is that mankind (and womankind) thinks that they are invincible and that we can do anything that we can *imagine* if we only pull up our *own* bootstraps, roll up our sleeves and apply the positive thinking principles.

## THE PRINCIPLES OF PRINCIPLES
1. an accepted or professed rule of action or conduct
2. a fundamental, primary, or general law or truth from which others are derived
3. a fundamental, primary, or general law or truth from which others are derived

4. a fundamental doctrine or tenet; a distinctive ruling opinion
5. a personal or specific basis of conduct or management
6. guiding sense of the requirements and obligations of right conduct
7. an adopted rule or method for application in action

*"Whatever the mind can conceive and believe, it can achieve."*
*Think and Grow Rich*
~Napoleon Hill

*Conceive* it, *believe* it, *achieve* it, *speak* it, *confess* it, *possess* it are all good things if the conception is given by God and you begin to think, speak, and act on the will of God in our lives. Again, when we take credit for any of these things as if we conjured them up we become humanist bordering on witchcraft (manipulating things) instead of God working in our lives.

Are you the master of your fate and the captain of your soul? Have you practiced the Frank Sinatra Theology of doing it *my way*? Another singer—one of my favorites, Elvis Presley—tried it his way and ended up dying on a toilet with a heart condition exacerbated by prescription medications abuse, *down at the end of lonely street at Heartbreak Hotel.* Have you pulled up your own bootstraps and become a self-made man or woman? Did you win the Rat Race finding out that you became the #1 Rat? Has your success turned out to be a failure, even though you were rich.

The problem with the P.M.A. (Positive Mental Attitude) proponents is that they don't submit to the *Lordship of Jesus the Christ.* Instead of "man is lord/a god "(little l and little g) they need to declare that "Jesus Christ is Lord" (Philippians 2:11).

JESUS: Iēsous (ee-ay-sooce')=Of Hebrew origin [H3091]; Jesus (that is, Jehoshua), the name of our Lord and two (three) other Israelites: - Jesus. H3091: yehôshûa yehôshûa (yeh-ho-shoo'-ah, yeh-ho-shoo'-ah) = Jehovah-saved; Jehoshua (that is, Joshua), the Jewish leader: - Jehoshua, Jehoshuah, Joshua.

> *"She (Mary) will bear (give birth) a son and you shall call His name Jesus for He will save His people from their sins."*
>
> ~Matthew 1:21

> *"And behold, you will conceive in your womb and bear a son, and you shall name Him, Jesus."*
>
> ~Luke 1:31

CHRIST: Christos (khris-tos')=From G5548; anointed, that is, the Messiah, an epithet of Jesus: - Christ.=G5548: chriō (khree'-o)=Probably akin to G5530 through the idea of contact; to smear or rub with oil, that is, (by implication) to consecrate to an office or religious service: - anoint. G5530: chraomai (khrah'-om-ahee)=Middle voice of a primary verb (perhaps rather from G5495, to handle); to furnish what is needed; (give an oracle, "graze" [touch slightly], light upon, etc.), that is, (by implication) to employ or (by extension) to act towards one in a given manner: - entreat, use. G5495: chasma (khas'-mah)= From a form of an obsolete primary "chao" (to "gape" or "yawn"); a "chasm" or vacancy (impassable interval): - gulf.

CHRIST: The Anointed One/The Messiah, anointed with the Holy Spirit and Power (dynamic ability). Jesus was anointed with yoke breaking, burden lifting, harassing and oppression removing healing power of the Holy Ghost for the purpose of destroying the works of the d-evil (Acts 10:38, Isaiah 10: 26, Luke 4:18-19, Isaiah 61:1-2, I John 3:8)

LORD: kurios (koo'-ree-os) =From kuros (supremacy); supreme in authority, that is, (as noun) controller; by implication Mr. (as a respectful title): - God, Lord, master, Sir.

It is not *"humans are in control/kurios/Lord"* but it is *"Jesus is in control/kurios."*

I personally love reading and listening to the various positive thinkers as opposed to the negative thinkers (negative stinkers, even some negative Christians). I believe that many of the *positive principles* that they believe and teach are actually Biblical principles, and these principles work for Christians and non-Christians alike, however, the P.M.A. minus the Lordship of Jesus equals good works that people think that it will give them favor with God and get them into heaven into the presence of the Father.

"If Adolph Hitler says the sky is blue it is. Truth is truth. It is a true statement." I'm not sure who said this, but my friend and fellow author and financial advisor Edwin McKnight (*Caius and the Great Troll Adventure*) reminded me of it.

> "*He saved us, not on the basis of deeds which we have done in righteousness, but (contrasted with deeds which we have done in righteousness) but according to His mercy, by the washing of regeneration and renewing by the Holy Spirit.*"
> ~Titus 3:5 emphasis mine

> "*For by* **grace** *you have been saved through faith; and that not of yourselves, it is the* gift of God; *not as a result of works, so that no one may boast, for we are His workmanship, created in Christ Jesus for works, which God prepared beforehand so that we should walk in them.*"
> ~Ephesians 2:8-10 emphasis mine

My hope, wish and desire is that you will be blessed (supremely happy and to be envied by others as they see you blessed) with these positive words. Of course, the lifestyle that I am talking about is a *lifestyle of love*. God himself demonstrates how to live this lifestyle.

> "*But God demonstrates His own love toward us in that while we were yet sinners Christ died for us.*"
> ~Romans 5:8

I have found that when our *"faith is towards (directional) God"* (Hebrews 6:1) and *"His power towards (directional) us"* (Ephesians

1:19), then that is when "His *SUPER* is on our *natural.*" Thanks and a Tip O Da Hat to Mylon LeFevre for the "His *SUPER* is on our *natural*" quote.

This is a *book of principles* that when applied in our lives, works! I believe that the principles will work for Christian and non-Christians alike because they are God-inspired. Oh, to be sure, if you have submitted to Jesus and His D.B.R. (death, burial, and resurrection), if you have made Jesus Christ your Lord, then things will flow better, and you will have even greater success along with peace that surpasses comprehension in all that you do (Philippians 4:6-19). But it is also sure that "through much tribulation, we enter the Kingdom of God," so you better have the principles of God with you as you "walk through the valley of the shadow of death," so you can keep on walking out of Shadow Valley (Psalm 23:4).

Rodney Boyd, 2021

## CHAPTER ONE

## JESUS IS LORD AND SAVIOR
### The Principle Of Salvation

The thing that separates the positive thinkers, those with a positive mental attitude (P.M.A.), those who follow the proponents of human possibility, and the followers of the secret of the law of attraction is the choice to be born again and the choice of making Jesus their Lord.

True enlightenment does not come by transcendental meditation, good works, inner human power, positive confession, or the human potential. True enlightenment comes from the light of the world, Jesus the Christ, the Anointed One, anointed with yoke-breaking, burden-lifting, and oppression-removing healing power of the Holy Ghost. The principles laid out in this book may work for someone who is *not* a Christian, *but* they will never fulfill the satisfaction and desire without Jesus.

It has been said that God has given us the power to make wealth.

> *"But you shall remember the LORD your God, for it is He who is giving you the power to make wealth, that He may confirm His covenant which He swore to your fathers, as it is this day."*
> ~Deuteronomy 8:18

The Lord your God just does not drop wealth into your life. The power and ability to make wealth is a confirmation of His covenant with us, which was an Old Testament principle that was fulfilled in Jesus.

At the same time, wealth does not necessarily bring happiness.

*"It is the blessing of the Lord that makes rich, And He adds no sorrow to it."*

~Pro-Verbs 10:22

Blessing means to be supremely happy and with life-joy and salvation as other are envious of what you've got. If you are rich and are in sorrow and not supremely happy, then it is not the blessing of the Lord but a situation of your own making.

One of the most mistaken views of a verse about money is that money is the root of all evil.

*"For the love (lust) of money is a root of all sorts of evil, and some by longing for it have wandered away from the faith and pierced themselves with many griefs."*

~I Timothy 6:10

Money is not the root of all sorts of evil. But the blessing of God when no sorrow is associated with it is the root of all kinds of goodness. It is the longing for money without the Lordship of Jesus that is the lure to wander away from true faith. Being pierced with many griefs is equal to sorrows added—and we know that when the Lord blesses,

*"He adds no sorrow to it."*

~Pro-Verbs 10:22

So, what brings us to the point of *walking in the principles of God* and not the principles of Rod (any human concept)?

CHAPTER TWO

## THE PRINCIPLES OF
### The Roman Road To Salvation

In 1970, my girlfriend, Brenda Williams, now my wife of 48+ years, led me to the Lord. We were discussing getting married, and I told her that we could raise the children in any religion she wanted, because I was a heathen, and I could adjust to any religion. She informed me that when she and the children died, they would go to heaven, and when I died I would be separated from them because I was lost and would go to hell. I guess this is what I get for dating a good Baptist girl who taught classes under trees in Child Evangelism. When she dropped that bombshell on me, I was in the middle of taking a bite from a delicious onion ring. I had been to church enough with her to realize that she was right. I took her home, pulled into her driveway, turned to her and said, "What do I have to do to get saved?" She then led me down the Roman Road to Salvation by memory, and then led me in a sinner's prayer. Here are the verses she told me about.

You must be born again. Jesus said that unless we are born again (born from above) that we cannot see or enter the Kingdom of God. (John 3:7) Remember we are talking about Kingdom Principles for living an abundant life

> "The thief cometh not, but for to steal, and to kill, and to destroy: I am come that they might have life and that they might have it more abundantly."
>
> ~John 10:10–KJV

You must realize that you are not righteous in your human self.

*"As it is written there is none righteous, not even one."*
~Romans 3:10, Psalm 13:1-3

You must realize that all have sinned and have fallen short of the glory of God. Yes, you try and try but the mission is not accomplished in your human abilities. You must realize that none=all, and that the cause and effect of none being righteous misses the mark of God's glory. Without God's glory, you just have your tarnished human potential.

*"For all have sinned (missed the mark of the target of glory) and fall short of the glory (His presence) of God"*
~Romans 3:23 addition mine

Wages is something you earn with human effort. Grace is getting what you don't deserve because of His divine influence on your heart (within) manifested outwardly (by what you do).

*"For the wages (something you earn from your own effort) of sin (missing the mark) is death, but the free gift (what you don't earn or deserve from your human effort) of God is eternal life in Christ Jesus our Lord."*
~Romans 6:23 addition mine

You must realize that justification and salvation is by His blood and not your human potential and works. It is all about Christ dying in you place more than about you deserving something.

*"But God demonstrates His own love toward us, in that while we were yet sinners, Christ died for us. Much more then, having now been justified by His blood, we shall be saved from the wrath of God through Him (Jesus)."*
~Romans 5:8-9 addition mine

You must realize that your salvation is hinged on what you confess (Jesus as Lord) and what you believe (God raised Him (Jesus) from the dead). The cause and effect is that you will be saved. You can't save yourself by your good works or your own sense of self-righteousness

> *"That if you confess (say the same thing as God, come into agreement with God with your mouth Jesus as Lord (kurios, the one in control), and believe (trust in, cling to, rely on, adhere to) your heart that God raised him from the dead, you will be saved."*
> ~Romans 10:9-10 addition mine

You must realize that this faith for salvation comes by hearing and hearing by the preached Word of God.

> *"So faith (for salvation) comes by hearing and hearing by the Word of God."*
> ~Romans 10:13 addition mine

The key to what was given to for salvation is in your heart and in your mouth.

> *"For whoever will call on the name of the Lord will be saved."*
> ~Romans 10:13

You must realize that it is the Word of Faith preached, and you receiving it by confessing with your mouth and believing in your heart that places you in the position to use the principles outlined in this book.

> *"But what does it (the righteousness of God)? The Word is near you, in your mouth and in your heart, that is the word of faith which we are preaching, that if you confess (come into agreement and say the same thing God says) with your mouth Jesus as Lord (kurios, in control) and believe (trust in, cling to, rely on, adhere to) that God raised Him from the dead (D.B.R.= Death, Burial, Resurrection, nothing more, nothing less), you will be saved for with the heart a*

*person believes resulting in (cause and effect of your mouth and your heart), in salvation (rescue or safety, physically or morally, deliver, health, salvation, save, saving)."*
~Romans 10:8-10 addition mine

Back in the fall of 1970, my lovely girlfriend shared the Roman Road to Salvation with me. then she led me in a sinner's prayer. My heart was primed to be saved. Here is a sample of the prayer. It may be my words, but it is your heart that will reveal the sincerity of your prayer.

> *Lord Jesus*
> *I am a sinner*
> *I need a Savior*
> *I confess with my mouth that you are Lord*
> *I believe with my heart that God raised You from the dead*
> *I confess with my mouth my sins and the need for a Savior*
> *I confess that I am saved not because of me but because of you*
> *In the name of Jesus, Amen.*

Now, you are ready to put into practice the principles of God for true success—and all the other things in the title of this book.

CHAPTER THREE

## THE WORD ABOUT WORDS

As a Speech-Language Pathologist, I love words. You have a syntax which is word order; semantics which is word meanings; pragmatics which is proper usage—all put together this forms our language, which is an agreed-upon code of how we communicate.

In this chapter, I want to go over the words that I have used in the title of this book. Some of the definitions will be from the Greek and/or Hebrew language, some will be from the dictionary, and others will be my spin on the word meanings. The book itself is a book on positive thinking with Jesus as Lord, the one in control of the good, bad, and ugly things in our lives.

**THINK POSITIVE INSTEAD OF THINKING NEGATIVE WHICH IS ALSO KNOWN AS THINKING LIKE A NEGATIVE THINKER STINKER**

The above statement is in large, black letters to emphasize the need for Positive Thinking.

*How* means the way that you do something and make it happen. The first word in the title of this book is *how*, so we will know *how* to apply these principles to accomplish what the title implies. We will now look at the *how* part to live a certain way to accomplish *the purposes of God in our lives.*

### DEFINITIONS

LIVE: bioō (bee-o'-o) = From G979; to spend existence: - live. G979: bios (bee'-os= A primary word; life, that is, (literally) the present state of existence; by implication the means of livelihood: - good, life, living.

LIVE: (1) to have life, as an organism; be alive; be capable of vital functions (2) to continue to have life; remain alive (Dictionary.com)

> *"I call heaven and earth to witness against you today, that I have set before you, life and death, the blessing and the curse. So choose life so that you may live, you and your descendants"*
> ~Deuteronomy 30:19

Yes, we have a choice in the matter of how we *live out our lives*. We have life/blessing, or we have death/curse. I like the fact that we are given a hint, a clue about which one to choose. *Choose Life*. I like the beer commercial with the most interesting man alive. He always ends the commercial with, *"choose wisely my friends."* The same goes for life—*"choose wisely my friends."*

Life is to be lived out loud. Life is more than just taking a breath and then exhaling it—life is living. To paraphrase Elvis Presley from his movie, *Loving You*, he's got a lot of living to do and he doesn't know who he would rather do it with than you.

I once shared Deuteronomy 30:19 with someone, and their response was, "Who would ever choose death or being cursed?" Man, wo-man, and humans do, but this book is going to encourage you to live a lifestyle of life and blessing.

MAXIMIZED: (1) to increase to the greatest possible amount or degree (2) to represent at the highest possible estimate; magnify. (3) to make the greatest or fullest use of.

The only other choice is to *minimize* the way you live your life. In my mind when I hear the word *minimize* in reference to my life, I hear the word *mediocrity*. In the Bible, Jesus tells us that our faith needs to be a minimum size to work, and that size is the size of a grain of mustard seed—the smallest seed around.

Here are just a few verses that speak of maximizing your life.

> *"And He said to them, "Because of the littleness of your faith; for truly I say to you, if you have faith the size of a mustard seed, you*

*will say to this mountain, 'Move from here to there,' and it will move, and* nothing will be impossible to you."
~Matthew 17:20 emphasis mine

That seed is not meant to stay small but to grow and not to regress. Seeds of faith can be smaller than a grain of mustard seed—small faith, large faith, no faith—but we are called to great faith.

"*...because your faith is* growing exceedingly (ever-increasing)..."
~II Thessalonians 1:3 emphasis mine

*"And my God will* liberally supply (fill to the full) *your every need according to His riches in glory in Christ Jesus."*
~Philippians 4:19–AMP emphasis mine

*"Now to him, that is able to do* exceeding abundantly above all that we ask or think, *according to the power that works in us."*
~Ephesians 3:21

*"Give, and [gifts] will be given to you;* good measure, pressed down, shaken together, and running over *will they pour into [the pouch formed by ] the bosom [of your robe and used as a bag]. For the measure you dealt out [with the measure you use when you confer benefits on others], it will be measured back to you."*
~Luke 6:38–AMP emphasis mine

OVERCOMING: nikaō (nik-ah'-o) = From G3529; to subdue (literally or figuratively): - conquer, overcome, prevail, get the victory. G3529: nikē (nee'-kay) =apparently a primary word; conquest (abstractly), that is, (figuratively) the means of success: - victory.

To overcome something means that there must be something to

overcome, obstacles, something or someone standing in our way to keep us from our full potential and vitality. Usually what is blocking our way is evil, caused by the d-evil, but many times it could just be something that happens in life.

> *"Do not be overcome by evil, but overcome evil with good."*
> ~Romans 12:21

VICTORIOUS: nikē (nee'-kay) = apparently a primary word; conquest (abstractly), that is, (figuratively) the means of success: - victory.

The old gospel song spoke of where our victory lies. We declare that there is Victory in Jesus! Sin, the law, the d-evil and his schemes along with his minions masked by human beings, try to have victory over us, but our victory is in Jesus. Read the principle of the Roman Road to Salvation again for full details about being in Jesus.

> *"The sting of death is sin and the power of sin is the law; but thanks be to God, who gives us the victory through our Lord Jesus the Christ, the Anointed One, anointed with yoke breaking, burden lifting, harassing and oppression removing power, by the Holy Ghost and power (duNAMis, dynamic ability)."*
> ~I Corinthians 15:56-57 with emphasis and addition mine.

MORE THAN A CONQUEROR: hupernikaō (hoop-er-nik-ah'-o) = to vanquish beyond, that is, gain a decisive victory: - more than conquer.

We are not just conquerors but *"more than conquerors."* A conqueror may conquer, but if we are more than conquerors there is no doubt about who wins. Someone can win a boxing match by split decision, but there will be doubt who is the conqueror. When there is a knockout—not a T.K.O. (technical knockout)—that winner is more than a conqueror.

ABUNDANT: perisseuō (***per-is-syoo'-o***)= to *superabound* (in quantity or quality), *be in excess, be superfluous*; also (transitively) to *cause to superabound* or *excel:* - (make, more) abound, (have, have more) abundance, (be more) abundant, be the better, enough and to spare, exceed, excel, increase, be left, redound, remain (over and above).

Abundance is enough to meet your needs and an overflow, enough left over to meet the needs of others. The thief (the d-evil) does everything he can to keep us in a poverty mentality by wrapping up that mindset into a religious package where we think poverty is the will of God for us.

> *"The thief comes only to steal and kill and destroy; I came that they may have life, and have it abundantly."*
> ~John 10:10

BLESSED: bârak (baw-rak')=A primitive root; to kneel; by implication to bless God (as an act of adoration), and (vice-versa) man (as a benefit); also (by euphemism) to curse (God or the king, as treason): - X abundantly, X altogether, X at all, blaspheme, bless, congratulate, curse, X greatly, X indeed, kneel (down), praise, salute, X still, thank.

> *"And God blessed them…"*
> ~Genesis 1:22

BLESSED: Makarios (mak-ar'-ee-os)=A prolonged form of the poetical makar (meaning the same); supremely blest; by extension fortunate, well off: - blessed, happy (X -ier).

> *"He (Jesus) opened His mouth and began to teach them saying, blessed…"*
> ~Matthew 5:1-11

Being blessed is a state of being because of your faith in the God of your provision. You believe (trust in, cling to, rely on and adhere to) Jesus as your Lord. The word *Lord* is from the Greek word "kurios" which means "the controller." The one in control for us He is in control of our blessings.

LORD: kurios (koo'-ree-os)=From kuros (supremacy); supreme in authority, that is, (as noun) controller; by implication Mr. (as a respectful title): - God, Lord, master, Sir.

FAVORED: chên (khane)=From H2603; graciousness, that is, subjectively (kindness, favor) or objectively (beauty): - favor, grace (-ious), pleasant, precious, [well-] favored. H2603: chânan (khaw-nan')= properly to bend or stoop in kindness to an inferior; to favor, bestow; causatively to implore (that is, move to favor by petition): - beseech, X fair, (be, find, shew) favor (-able), be (deal, give, grant (gracious (-ly), intreat, (be) merciful, have (shew) mercy (on, upon), have pity upon, pray, make supplication, X very.

PROSPEROUS: tsâlach tsâlêach (tsaw-lakh', tsaw-lay'-akh)=A primitive root; to push forward, in various senses (literally or figuratively, transitively or intransitively): - break out, come (mightily), go over, be good, be meet, be profitable, (cause to, effect, make to, send) prosper (-ity, -ous, -ously). (Joshua 1:8)

PROSPEROUS: per-is-sos'= (in the sense of beyond); superabundant (in quantity) or superior (in quality); by implication excessive; adverb (with G1537) violently; neuter (as noun) preeminence: - exceeding abundantly above, more abundantly, advantage, exceedingly, very highly, beyond measure, more, superfluous, vehement [-ly].

> *"So you will find favor and good report, in the sight of God and man."*
> ~Pro-Verb 3:2

> *"This book of the law shall not depart from your mouth, but you shall meditate on it day and night, so that you may be careful to do*

*according to all that is written in it; for then you will make your way prosperous, and then you will have success."*
~Joshua 1:8

PROSPER: euodoō (yoo-od-o'-o)= to help on the road, that is, (passively) succeed in reaching; figuratively to succeed in business affairs: - (have a) prosper (-ous journey).

*"Beloved, I pray that in all respects you may prosper and be in good health, just as your soul prospers."*
III John 3

SUCCESSFUL: śâkal (saw-kal')=A primitive root; to be (causeatively make or act) circumspect and hence intelligent: - consider, expert, instruct, prosper, (deal) prudent (-ly), (give) skill (-ful), have good success, teach, (have, make to) understand (-ing), wisdom, (be, behave self, consider, make) wise (-ly), guide wittingly.

*"This book of the Law shall not depart out of your mouth, but you shall meditate (ruminate, mutter under your breath) on it day and night, that you may observe and do according to all that is written in it. For then you shall make your way prosperous, and then you shall deal wisely and have good success."*
~Joshua 1:8 (AMP) addition mine

LIFESTYLE: The habits, attitudes, tastes, moral standards, economic level, etc., that together constitute the mode of living of an individual or group.

*"Keep your behavior excellent among the Gentiles, so that in the thing in which they slander you as evildoers, they may because of your good deeds, as they observe them, glorify God in the day of visitation."*
~I Peter 2:12

*"Only conduct yourselves in a manner worthy of the gospel of Christ, so that whether I come and see you or remain absent, I will*

*hear of you that you are standing firm in one spirit, with one mind striving together for the faith of the gospel; in no way alarmed by your opponents—which is a sign of destruction for them, but of salvation for you, and that too, from God."*
~Philippians 1:27-28

*"Therefore I, the prisoner of the Lord, implore you to* walk in a manner (lifestyle) *worthy of the calling with which you have been called, being diligent to preserve the unity of the Spirit in the bond of peace."*
~Ephesians 4:2-3 addition mine

So there you have *the vocabulary* of *God's will for our life.* The d-evil will try and twist the words just like he twisted the Word of God as he was trying to tempt Jesus in the wilderness. The only problem—well not the *only* problem—was that Jesus:
1. Knew the Word of God.
2. Had the Holy Spirit at the beginning of entering the wilderness, being led about in the wilderness by the Holy Spirit.
3. Knew His authority and knew how to use that authority.
4. Came out the other side of the temptation full of the power of the Spirit. (Matthew 4:1-11, Luke 4:1-14)

For us to live the maximized, overcoming, more than conqueror, abundant, blessed, prosperous, successful lifestyle we must submit to the Lordship (control) of Jesus, crucify the flesh (our carnal nature where we are in control) and allow the Holy Spirit to flow out us like rivers of living water. When we do those things, there is nothing that we face in the world that can keep us from that lifestyle. In the next few chapters, we will be learning the principles that will exemplify the title of the book in our lives.

CHAPTER FOUR

## THE KINGDOM PRINCIPLE

To have a maximized, overcoming, more than conqueror, victorious, blessed, successful, abundant, prosperous, successful lifestyle you have to *have a firm foundation*. This is what I call *a Kingdom Foundation*. To have a Kingdom, there must be a King, and there must be subjects who yield their will to the King willingly. In your typical book about living a prosperous and successful lifestyle, they also speak of a kingdom (little k) where the human being is the king. While we were designed by God with capabilities, we cannot obtain a true maximized, overcoming, more than conqueror, victorious, blessed, abundant, prosperous, successful lifestyle unless the king is submitted to the King.

KINGDOM: basileia (bas-il-i'-ah)=From G935; properly royalty, that is, (abstractly) rule, or (concretely) a realm (literally or figuratively): - kingdom, + reign. G935: basileus (bas-il-yooce')=Probably from G939 (through the notion of a foundation of power); a sovereign (abstractly, relatively or figuratively): - king. G939: basis (bas'-ece)=From bainō (to walk); a pace ("base"), that is, (by implication) the foot: - foot.

When you extrapolate the definitions from the definition we see that a Kingdom and the King is:
1. Royalty
2. Rule
3. Realm
4. Reign
5. Foundation of power

6. Sovereign
7. Pace (base)
8. Foot

The first thing you need to realize about God's Kingdom and the world's kingdom (with a human king) is that God's Kingdom is *based on a covenant*. Where there is an agreement between two powers and an animal sacrifice is made by the cutting to pieces of the animal with much bloodshed, and the parties walk between the cut pieces, it is called cutting of the covenant. There are many types of covenants found in the Bible, but the covenant that we will look at is known as the Suzerain Treaty.

SUZERAIN: (1) a sovereign or a state exercising political control over a dependent state. (2) A feudal (relating to, or like the feudal system, or its political, military, social, and economic structure) overlord. (Dictionary.com)

A *Suzerain treaty* is where a higher power (king) offers the conditions of the treaty to a lower power (king), where the lower king cannot bring anything to the table other than acceptance of the conditions of the higher power (king). This is the type of treaty/covenant that we (the lower no power) have with God (the higher power). The Father God (Godfather), "makes us an offer we can't refuse."

> "And on His robe and on His thigh He has a name written, "KING OF KINGS, AND LORD OF LORDS."
> ~Revelation 19:6

Yes, there is a Kingdom and there is a King.

Jesus' name (the King of kings and the Lord of lords) is above all names that are named. This name, Jesus, is above the names of dis-eases, situations, circumstances, political entities, world leaders and economics.

> "For this reason also God highly exalted Him, and bestowed on Him the name which is above every name which is above every

*name, so (the reason for the exaltation and bestowing) at the name of Jesus every knee will bow of those who are in heaven and on earth and under the earth, and that every tongue will confess that Jesus Christ is Lord to the glory of God the Father."*
~Philippians 2:9-11

This is where you and me submit to the King as we accept His Suzerain treaty. The phrase in Philippians 2:9, *"For this reason"* refers to how he was exalted and bestowed on Him the *"name which is above every name (that is named)."* When you read Philippians 2:1-8 you will see not only how Jesus was exalted, but how we can be exalted also. The key is what Gayle Erwin, author of *The Jesus Style*, points out and is what I call, The Humility Principle. The Humility Principle is how you live out The Kingdom Principle.

*"Therefore if there is any encouragement in Christ, if there is any consolation of love, if there is any fellowship of the Spirit, if any affection and compassion, make my joy complete…"*
1. Be of the same mind
2. Maintain the same love
3. Be united in spirit
4. Be intent on one purpose
5. Do nothing from selfishness
6. Do nothing from empty conceit
7. Have humility of mind
8. Regard one another as more important than yourselves
9. Do not merely look out for your own personal interest
~Philippians 2:1 (addition and emphasis mine

If you are going to live a maximized, overcoming, more than a conqueror, victorious, blessed, abundant, prosperous, and successful lifestyle, you will have to accept the conditions of the King and the principles of His Kingdom.

When Jesus was walking around on planet Earth, He spent the last three years of His life pre-Death, Burial, and Resurrection, proclaiming the Gospel (Good News) of the Kingdom of God and then demonstrating the Kingdom of God on earth as it is in heaven.

This thing called the Kingdom of God is not made of meat or drink, or financial windfalls, or economic gurus, or political entities, and definitely not flesh and blood here on planet Earth.

> *"[After all] the Kingdom (rule, reign, foundation of power) of God is not a matter of [getting the] food and drink [one likes], but instead it is righteousness (that state which makes a person acceptable to God) and [heart] peace (all whole and at rest) and joy (cheerfulness and calm delight) in the Holy Spirit (Ghost)."*
> ~Romans 14:17 AMP with additions and emphasis mine

When Jesus is delivering His teaching on the Mount (Matthew 5:1–48, Matthew 6:1–34, Matthew 7:1–29) He speaks of the provision of the Lord. The provision of the Lord is based on the supply of the Lord found in Christ Jesus and the glory of God.

> *"And My God will liberally supply (fill to the full) your every need according to (based on) His riches in glory in Christ Jesus."*
> ~Philippians 4:19 AMP, emphasis and addition mine

Jesus emphasizes that no one can serve two masters. (Matthew 6:24) You will either:
1. hate one
2. love the other
3. stand by one
4. despise and be against the other

Jesus then underscores that you cannot serve God and mammon (deceitful riches, money, possessions, or whatever is trusted in—see Matthew 6:24, The Amplified Bible.)

I like that phrase, "or whatever is trusted in." Who you trust is your Lord.

LORD: kurios (koo'-ree-os)=From kuros (supremacy); supreme in authority, that is, (as noun) controller; by implication Mr. (as a respectful title): - God, Lord, master, Sir.

If you are going to walk in the Kingdom of God, Jesus must be your King and Lord. If you trust in anyone or thing other than Jesus, then that thing or person is the *kurios*, the one who is supreme in authority, the controller (the one in control of every aspect of your life), and your Master.

Let me underscore once again, if you are going to live a maximized, overcoming, more than conqueror, victorious, blessed, abundant, prosperous, successful lifestyle, you are going to have to submit to the Lord of the Kingdom principle.

As Jesus is teaching the principles of the Kingdom in the Sermon on the Mount (some say the principles are the constitution of the Kingdom), He lays out how the Kingdom of God relates to the economy of the Kingdom which when the principles are applied by faith, affects the things on earth as it is in heaven. (Matthew 6:10)

Here on earth we store up things in banks, warehouses, 401ks, retirement funds. Jesus specifically says don't store up these things on earth.

> *"Do not store up for yourselves treasures on earth, where moth and rust destroy, and where thieves break in and steal."*
> ~Matthew 6:18

In contrast Jesus give another perspective of storing riches.

> *"But (in contrast to) store up for yourselves treasures in heaven, where neither moth nor rust destroys, and where thieves do not break in our steal; for where your treasure is, there your heart will also be."*
> ~Matthew 6:19

Greed is a matter of the heart when you hoard treasures as if you will miss out if you don't watch out for yourself. Again, God is not against wisdom, wise spending, preparing your life utilizing the principles of sowing and reaping, reciprocity, and meeting the needs of the poor.

> *"No servant can serve two master; for either he will hate the*

*one and love the other, or else he will be devoted to one and despise the other. You cannot serve God (His Kingdom) and wealth (your kingdom)."*
>             ~Luke 16:13, with emphasis and addition mine

The basics of life on planet Earth are covered by Kingdom principles, so there is no need to worry (be anxious). (Matthew 6:25, Philippians 4:6)
- Your life
- Eating
- Drinking
- Your Body
- Clothes you put on

"…is not life more than food, and body more than clothing?"

The answer is a resounding yes, but He is not saying, "Don't buy food, stop eating, stop drinking, go around naked."

> *"The Kingdom of God is not meat or drink but righteousness, peace and joy in the Holy Ghost."*
>                              ~Romans 14:17

"The kingdom of man IS meat, drink, money, wealth, storehouses, etc. and is manifested in unrighteousness, anxiety and depression." (Romans 14:17 with new twist mine)

Jesus uses nature as the example of not worrying about stuff. The birds don't sow, they don't reap or even gather into barns, and yet your heavenly Father feeds them. Hey, guess what? You are worth much more than birds! You cannot worry and add anything to your life. (Matthew 6:27) Worrying about food, clothes, and the stuff of life is not worth it when God is in the food and clothing business with nature and with you. (Matthew 6:28-29)

When you worry about stuff, you are revealing your faith level—which is little faith. God expects us to have faith at least the size of a mustard seed, but when we worry our faith is smaller than a mustard seed-size faith. God expects there to be growth in our faith from no faith, to mustard seed faith, to great faith, to ever increasing faith. He does not expect us to have a regression of faith to little faith, smaller than a grain of mustard seed.

Gentiles worry and seek stuff, but our heavenly Father know that you need these things even before you ask.

> *"So do not be like them (religious hypocrites, Pharisees, religious leaders) for your Father know what you need before you ask him."*
> ~Matthew 6:8 addition mine

So, what are we to do? I am glad that you asked. I believe that to live the maximized, overcoming, more than conqueror, victorious, blessed, abundant, prosperous, and successful lifestyle, is hinged on us seeking His Kingdom (rule, reign, foundations of power).

> *But seek first his Kingdom and His righteousness, and all these things (stuff) shall be added to you. So do not worry about tomorrow; for tomorrow will take care for itself. Each day has enough trouble of its own."*
> ~Matthew 6:33-34 addition mine

Remember we have said that God is *not against wealth* or having things here on planet Earth.

> *"But you shall* remember the Lord your God, *for it is He who is giving you power to make wealth that* He may confirm *His covenant which He swore to your fathers, as it is this day."*
> ~Deuteronomy 8:18, emphasis mine

> *"It is the blessing of the Lord that makes rich, and He adds no sorrow to it (the blessing of riches)."*
> ~Pro-Verbs 10:22 addition mine

God does not bless greed and neither does He condemn the blessing of wealth and riches. God is pro-prosperity and pro-success. (Joshua 1:8, III John 1:2)

## SEEING AND ENTERING THE KINGDOM TO PRACTICE EFFECTIVE KINGDOM PRINCIPLES ON EARTH AS IT IS IN HEAVEN

Jesus, the Word, who was with God and was God and became flesh and dwelt among us here on planet Earth (John 1:1-14) met with a man of the Pharisees by night named Nicodemus. I will refer to him as "Nick at Night," aka Nick, based on the T.V. channel that shows old T.V. shows.

Nick was a ruler of the Jews. Remember that Jesus was a Jew who was upsetting the religious leaders to the point of them wanting to murder Him to get rid of the threat of His Kingdom taking over.

> *"And this man came to Jesus by night and said to Him 'Rabbi, we know that You have come from God as a teacher; for no one can do these signs (miracles) that You do unless God is with Him.'"*
> ~John 3:2

SIGNS/MIRACLES: sēmeion (say-mi'-on)=Neuter of a presumed derivative of the base of G4591; an indication, especially ceremonially or supernaturally: - miracle, sign, token, wonder.

Jesus then clarifies for Nick about the Kingdom (where He was the King).

> *"Jesus answered and said to him, "Truly, truly (whenever you get two truly it is time to listen up), I say to you (Nick at Night), unless one is born again (born anew, born from above) he cannot see the Kingdom of God."*
> ~John 3:4, emphasis and addition mine

SEE: eidō (i'-do)= properly to see (literally or figuratively); by implication (in the perfect only) to know: - be aware, behold, X can (+ not tell), consider, (have) known (-ledge), look (on), perceive, see, be sure, tell, understand, wist, wot.

The prerequisite to experience this Kingdom of God is to see it first. This happens when we are "born again, born anew, born from above" (and not a physical birth here on planet Earth).

BORN: gennaō (ghen-nah'-o)= to procreate (properly of the father, but by extension of the mother); figuratively to regenerate: - bear, beget, be born, bring forth, conceive, be delivered of, gender, make, spring.

AGAIN: anōthen (an'-o-then)=From G507; from above; by analogy from the first; by implication anew: - from above, again, from the beginning (very first), the top. G507: anō (an'-o)=; upward or on the top: - above, brim, high, up.

This book has been *laying out principles* that if followed you will *experience true Biblical Success*. Even those who are not born again and not only cannot see the Kingdom of God but cannot even enter the Kingdom of God, can experience the cause and effect of the principles of the Kingdom, but if you are born again—if by faith you hear and obey his commandments/principles and love the Lord—you will experience His love and manifestation, disclosure, and revelation. There are many unbelieving people who demonstrate more of the fruit of the Spirit in their lives than some born again and Spirit-filled Christians.

> *"The person who has My commands and keeps them is the one who [really] loves Me; and whoever [really] loves Me will be loved by My Father, and I [too] will love him and will show (disclose, reveal, manifest) Myself to him. (I will let Myself be clearly seen by him and make Myself real to him.]"*
> ~John 14:21 AMP, with additions and emphasis mine

I believe that this disclosure, this revelation, this manifestation is being able to see the Kingdom of God and the King clearly.

As with any good question and answer session, more questions arise.

Nick at Night said to Him, "How can a man be born when he is old? He cannot enter a second time into his mother's womb and be born, can he?"

I believe this is a valid question if you are asking from a human standpoint. Sometimes the things and principles of the Kingdom just don't make any sense to the natural mind.

> *"But a natural man (like Nick at Night) does not accept the thing of the Spirit of God, for they are foolishness to him (like being born a second time); and he cannot understand them, because they are spiritually appraised."*
> ~I Corinthians 2:4 addition mine

Jesus throws another *truly, truly* on Nick.

> *"Jesus answered, truly, truly, I say to you, unless one is born of water and the Spirit he cannot enter into the Kingdom of God."*
> ~John 3:5

ENTER: eiserchomai (ice-er'-khom-ahee)= to enter (literally or figuratively): - X arise, come (in, into), enter in (-to), go in (through).

Jesus is speaking of two types of birth:
1. a physical birth where a baby is born after the water sac is broken
2. a spiritual birth by The Holy Spirit

The first birth brings a human being into the physical realm, and the second birth brings the human being into the Kingdom realm where you not only *see* the Kingdom but you *enter* the Kingdom of God.

Jesus further clarifies this being born again concept.

> *"That which is born of the flesh is flesh, and that which is born of the Spirit is spirit."*
> John 3:6

Being born of the flesh brings forth flesh (human birth) via the water from the water sac being broken. Being born of the Spirit (from on high) brings alive the human spirit which was dead from sin because of the high treason of Adam and Eve. (Genesis 3:1-24, Romans 5:12, II Corinthians 5:14-21)

Nick at Night was amazed. Jesu told Him not to be amazed that He had told him that he must be born again, born anew, born from above and not just born in the physical human stage.

Jesus then gives Nick a beautiful example of the Spirit of God blowing. I have used this with my atheist friends who say they cannot believe in anything that they could not see and explain. Why? Because they are humanist who believe that they are the gods who are in control of their lives. Thinking that there is a Holy Spirit or God or Jesus is a foreign concept to them.

*"The wind blows where it wishes and you hear the sound of it, but do not know where it comes from and where it is going; so is everyone who is born of the Spirit (born again, born anew, born from above)."*
John 3:8 addition mine

I ask my atheist friends to take a deep breath (and they do) and then blow it out again (and they do). I then ask them if they saw the breath or can they explain the principles of respiratory. Usually, they can't, and that is when I tell them that is like the Spirit, you can't see him but you can see *His effects* in your life. On a cold winter day, you can see your breath, and so it is in this cold world that we live—we can see the move of the Spirit.

Again, one question, one answer leads to another question from Nick.

*"Nicodemus said to Him, 'how can these things be?"*
~John 3:9

Jesus response to Nicks "how can these things be" is to ask,

*"How can you not understand these thing being a teacher of Israel.*
~John 3:10

Jesus was merely testifying what He knows, but Nick had not

accepted Jesus testimony. (John 3:11) If Jesus spoke to Nick of earthly things and he could not understand them, how would he believe heavenly things? (John 3:12)

Jesus then closes out his conversation with Nick at Night by bringing the conversation around to His Death, Burial, Resurrection and John 3:16.

> *"For God (who Nick could not see) so loved the world (including Nick) that He (the Father) gave (sacrificed) His only begotten Son (Jesus) that whosoever believes (trusts in, clings to, relies on, adheres to) Him (Jesus, whom Nick was having this night conversation with) should not perish die a physical death) but have everlasting life (seeing and entering the Kingdom)."*
>
> ~John 3:16 addition mine

As we continue to study how to live a maximized, overcoming, more than conqueror, victorious, blessed, abundant, prosperous, successful lifestyle we will study what I call *Kingdom Principles*.

CHAPTER FIVE

## THE PRAYER PRINCIPLE

Prayer in its basic form is merely talking with the Creator of the universe with an expectancy that He would talk back to his Creation. In the natural, communication is interaction between two human beings who are equipped with a receiver and transmitter. The communication is based on a code that both parties understands. At times there may be a disturbance in the frequency where there is static impeding the understanding of what is being communicated.

I know that as a child, I would be in bed, supposedly asleep, and I will be attempting to listen to W.L.S. radio out of Chicago. I would be under my covers trying to tune out the static and tune in the music. When I finally turned the dial to a certain position, I could hear crystal clear, music from Chicago. So it is with prayer; we must be tuned into the frequency of heaven to hear the voice of God that will line up with the communications code manual, the Bible.

For more detail on this communication system in the natural and in the Supernatural check out my book entitled *Speaking and Hearing the Word of God (A Speech-Language Pathologist's Perspective)*. I will outline this communication system here also.

Communication begins with a thought where that thought is expressed either verbally, written, or in sign language. Language is an agreed upon code by which we communicate. Once the thought is formulated, there is an inhalation of oxygen that passes through the vocal folds (cords) that draws the folds together by a principle called the Bernoulli Effect. This is much like standing in a shower and as the steam rises, if you get close to the shower curtain it is brought to your skin. So it is when this air passes through the vocal folds and closes them tightly. Then as the air is released, it breaks apart the closed vocal folds and sets into motion vibrations at a certain frequency. As the sound goes through the resonating cavities (including the throat, the nasal cavity, and the mouth. The mouth then forms the word and produces the thoughts that are sent the receiver.

The sound now travels through the air and makes contact with the human receiver via the flaps on the side of the head called the auricle or the pinna. Some think these bilateral flaps are our ears but they are merely collectors of sound that guides the sound vibrations down the ear canal which leads to the tympanic membrane (the eardrum). The sound then sets into motion three bones in the middle ear including the malleus (hammer), the incus (anvil), and stapes (stirrup).

The synergistic quality of the three bones takes the sound waves and turns the sound into a mechanical chain that is hooked into the inner ear (the cochlea shaped like a snail). There is liquid that is set into motion in the cochlea in the inner ear (hydraulic) that goes in and out, round and back to the origin at the foot plate at the juncture between the middle and inner ear. Along the cochlea there are tiny hairs connected (cilia) that snap when the fluid crosses over the hairs that sends electric impulses of a certain frequency to the VIII Cranial Nerve (the Acoustic Nerve) that tells the brain what you just heard.

Then the human decodes what was heard and encodes a response back to the other human receiver. This is what we call communication. Have I mentioned that we are fearfully and wonderfully made by the Creator of the universe?

> *"For You formed my inward parts; You wove me in my mother's womb. I will give thanks to You, for I am fearfully and wonderfully made; Wonderful are your works, and my soul knows it very well."*
> Psalm 139:13-14

As much as we desire to communicate with one another, the Father desires to communicate with us and for us to communicate with

Him. This is essential for these principles that we will be studying as we walk by faith and not by sight.

*Prayer is the principle of communication.*

## CHAPTER SIX

## THE FAITH PRINCIPLE

Everything flows out of faith towards God. (Hebrews 6:1) This thing called faith works by love. (Galatians 5:6) When our faith is towards (directed towards) God (Hebrews 6:1) and His power is directed towards us who believes (Ephesians 1:19) that is where, as Mylon Lefevre (Gospel singer and teacher of the Word) says, "When His *SUPER* comes on our *natural*."

> *"The principles in this book about living the maximized, overcoming, more than a conqueror, victorious, blessed, abundant, successful and prosperous life style must be walked out by faith and not by sight differently than those who walk by doubt and fear."*
> ~Rodfucious

NOTE: Rodfucious is my secret persona who espouses, quirky wit and wisdom about life.

This thing called faith is defined in Hebrews 11:1.

> *"Now faith is the assurance (the confirmation, the title deed) of the things [we] hope for, being the proof of things [we] do not see and the conviction of their reality [faith perceiving as real fact what is not revealed to the senses."*
> ~Hebrews 11:1 (AMP)

FAITH: pistis (pis'-tis)=From G3982; persuasion, that is, credence; moral conviction (of religious truth, or the truthfulness of God or a religious teacher), especially reliance upon Christ for salvation;

abstractly constancy in such profession; by extension the system of religious (Gospel) truth itself: - assurance, belief, believe, faith, fidelity. G3982: peithō (pi'-tho)=A primary verb; to convince (by argument, true or false); by analogy to pacify or conciliate (by other fair means); reflexively or passively to assent (to evidence or authority), to rely (by inward certainty): - agree, assure, believe, have confidence, be (wax) content, make friend, obey, persuade, trust, yield.

> *"Now faith is the substance/assurance of things hope (confidently expected) the conviction/evidence of things not seen."*
> ~Hebrews 11:1 addition mine

In reference to *living a lifestyle*, as a righteous man who was made righteous by Jesus, it must be *lived by faith*.

> *"For in the Gospel, a righteousness which God ascribes is revealed, both springing from faith and leading to faith [disclosed through the way of faith that arouses to more faith]. As it is written, the man who through faith is just and upright shall live and shall live by faith."*
> ~Romans 1:17, Habakkuk 2:4, Galatians 3:1, Hebrew's 10:38 addition mine

When you see four references to living (a lifestyle) by faith, you get the idea that faith is necessary to live with style. According to Hebrews 11:1 in the Amplified Bible, faith is:

- Substance/Assurance: hupostasis (hoop-os'-tas-is)= a setting under (support), that is, (figuratively) concretely essence, or abstractly assurance (objectively or subjectively): - confidence, confident, person, substance.
- Confirmation: (1) To establish the truth, accuracy, validity, or genuineness of; corroborate (2) To acknowledge with definite assurance (3) to make valid or binding by some formal or legal act; sanction; ratify (4) to make firm or more firm; add strength to; settle or establish firmly (5) to strengthen (a person) in habit, resolution, opinion (dictionary.com)

- Title Deed: a deed or document containing or constituting evidence of ownership (dictionary.com)
- Hope: elpizō (el-pid'-zo)= From G1680; to expect or confide: - (have, thing) hope (-d) (for), trust. G1680: elpis (el-pece')=- From elpō which is a primary word (to anticipate, usually with pleasure); expectation (abstract or concrete) or confidence: - faith, hope. (confident expectation)
- Proof/Evidence: elegchos (el'-eng-khos)=From G1651; proof, conviction: - evidence, reproof. G1651: elegchō (el-eng'-kho)=Of uncertain affinity; to confute, admonish: - convict, convince, tell a fault, rebuke, reprove.
- Things: elegchō (el-eng'-kho)=Of uncertain affinity; to confute, admonish: - convict, convince, tell a fault, rebuke, reprove.
- Do Not See: blepō (blep'-o)=A primary verb; to look at (literally or figuratively): - behold, beware, lie, look (on, to), perceive, regard, see, sight, take heed.
- Conviction: (1) a fixed or firm belief (2) the state of being convinced.
- Reality: (1) The state or quality of being real (2) resemblance to what is real (3) real things, facts, or events taken as a whole; state of affairs (dictionary.com)
- Perceiving As Real Fact: (1) to become aware of, know, or identify by means of the senses (2) to recognize, discern, envision, or understand
- That Which Is Not Revealed: (1) to make known; disclose; divulge (2) to lay open to view; display; exhibit
- The Senses: sight, hearing, smell, taste, and touch (livescience.com)

One of the problems that happens as we try to live our lives, live out our lifestyle, is our senses can easily be swayed. When we *walk by sight and not by faith* we begin to believe (trust in, cling to, rely on, adhere) to the wrong thing that we see, hear, touch, smell and feel. That is why we must walk by faith and not by sight. (II Corinthians 5:7)

*"For we walk by faith [we regulate our lives and conduct ourselves*

*by our conviction or belief respecting man's relationship to God and divine things, with trust and holy fervor; thus we walk" not by sight or appearance."*
~II Corinthians 5:7 (AMP)

It is hard to separate the *living by faith* and *the way we walk*.

LIVE: bioō (bee-o'-o) = From G979; to spend existence: - live. G979: bios (bee'-os= A primary word; life, that is, (literally) the present state of existence; by implication the means of livelihood: - good, life, living.

WALK: peripateō (per-ee-pat-eh'-o)= to tread all around, that is, walk at large (especially as proof of ability); figuratively to live, deport oneself, follow (as a companion or votary): - go, be occupied with, walk (about).

## BEGINNINGS OF OUR FAITH

When Jesus had cleansed the temple of money changers (Mark 11:1-20-21), he was returning to Bethany, and they passed by a fig tree that Jesus sought out some fruit, but there was no fruit on the tree. Jesus spoke to the tree and declared, "May no one ever eat fruit from you again." (Mark 11:14) When they passed the tree Peter took note of the tree. "Rabbi, look the tree which You cursed has withered (from the roots up)." (Mark 11:20-21)

Jesus made a statement that He would use to springboard into a teaching on prayer (that we will cover later in the book)

*"And Jesus answered (Peter) saying to them, Have faith in God constantly."*
~Mark 11:22 (AMP)

Two things I noticed with this verse,
1. He told them to have faith. If He expected them to have this thing called faith, He must provide them the means which to get it.

2. This thing called faith that they were to have was not just a one time or intermittent thing to have, it was to be constant, 7/24/365, in every situation and circumstance.

We are not born with faith. Faith comes from somewhere and to someone. Faith comes as a result of cause and effect. Someone preaches, teaches, and shares the witness about Jesus the Christ and the good news of the Gospel which is about the death, burial, and resurrection of Jesus. Years ago (back in the 1970s) in Bible School (Tennessee Temple Bible School) I learned about the Gospel (Good News) in a nutshell. It was a thumbnail sketch distilled down to the basics.

> *"Now I make know to you, brethren, the gospel which I preached to you which also you received, in which also you stand, by which you were also saved, if you hold fast the word which I preached to you, unless you believed in vain."*
>
> ~I Corinthians 15:1-2

The Word is preached, you receive, and you stand in what you received (believed), and the cause and effect is that you are saved.

For I delivered to you as of first importance what I also received, that Christ died for our sins according to the Scriptures, and that He was buried and that He was raised on the third day according to the Scriptures (D.B.R.= Death, Burial, Resurrection, nothing more and nothing less). (I Corinthians 15:3-4)

> *"And that He appeared (alive) to Cephas (Peter), then to the twelve. After that He appeared (alive) to more than five hundred brethren at one time, most of whom remain until now, but some have fallen asleep (died); then He appeared to James, and then to all the apostles; and last of all, at to one untimely born, He appeared to me (Paul) also."*
>
> ~I Corinthians 15:5-8

NOTE: This is what Paul was talking about when he says the preachers preach; they were preaching about the death, burial, and resurrection of Jesus. This is the turning point of not having faith (that Jesus said we should have constantly) and then faith coming by hearing and hearing by the Word of God/concerning Christ/Words of Christ.

*"So faith comes from hearing, and hearing by the word of Christ."*
~Romans 10:17

*"Whoever calls on the name of the Lord will be saved."*
~Romans 10:13

The question is:

*"How will they call on Him in whom they have not believed? How will they believe in Him whom they have not heard? And how will they hear without a preacher? How will they preach unless they are sent?"*
~Romans 10:14-15

So, again, Jesus tells his followers that they must have this thing called faith, constantly ,and now we see that He not only requires faith but provides the means by which we can get faith. To me this is crucial, not only for salvation but also for everything in our lives. We are called to live by faith (Romans 1:17) and called to walk out our existence by faith. (II Corinthians 5:7)

Remember that all of mankind was unrighteous. There was none righteous, no not one. (Romans 3:10) All (every last single human being) have sinned and fallen short of the glory of God. (Romans 6:23) Paul (the guy who wrote Romans) also tells us that those who are righteous shall live by faith. (Romans 1:17) So, something happened between none are righteous, and the righteous shall live by faith. Well, apparently faith came, and that faith was in the death, burial and resurrection of Jesus. What happened is revealed in II Corinthians 5:21.

*"He (Father God) made Him (Jesus) who knew no sin to be sin on*

*our behalf (on the cross) so (cause and effect) that we might become the righteousness of God in Him (in Him we are righteous, outside of Him not righteous no not one)."*
~II Corinthians 5:21 addition mine

Romans 10 speaks of righteousness based on the Law of Moses and how those who practice righteousness based on the Law will have to live (a lifestyle). (Romans 10:4) People try to establish their own righteousness, but they don't subject themselves to the righteousness of God. They don't understand that Christ (Jesus) is the end of the law for this thing called righteousness to everyone (whosoever) believes (trusts in, clings to, relies on and adheres to) Jesus and His death, burial and resurrection. (Romans 10:1-5)

So faith comes by hearing and hearing by the Word of God/Christ. But faith without works (doing something, corresponding actions) is of none effect (dead, D.O.A., dead on arrival). (James 2:17)

This new found righteousness has a language of its own. It (the righteous person) speaks a certain way.

*"But the righteousness based on faith speaks as follows: Do not say (speak) in your heart, who will ascend into heaven? (That is to bring Christ down), or who will descend into the abyss? (That is, to bring Christ up from the dead)."*
~Romans 10:6 addition mine

So, after you believed and faith comes to you, what do you do with it (faith). What does a righteousness based on faith say (speak)? Well, I'm glad you asked.

## SPEECH PATTERNS

What you think and believe will be revealed in your words and speech patterns.

The righteousness based on faith says:

*"The word is near you, in your mouth (the oral cavity with your teeth, gums, lips) and in your heart (not the physical pump of the*

*body but the core, center, your human spirit, you innermost being/belly) (not up in heaven or down in the abyss but in your mouth)..."*
~Romans 10:8 addition mine

The word that you speak is called the Word of Faith. This Word of Faith is the same word that the preachers are preaching by which faith came to you.

NOTE: This thing called The Word of Faith is essential for salvation but is only the beginning as you live (a lifestyle) by faith (Romans 1:17) and you walk (regulate yourself and conduct yourself) not by sight but by faith. (II Corinthians 5:7) It is by faith that you believe for healing, believe for your emotional needs, believe for your financial needs, and believes for every area of your life.

Romans 10:9-11 speaks of how you will not be disappointed.

DISAPPOINTED/ASHAMED: kataischunō (kat-ahee-sk-hoo'-no)= to shame down, that is, disgrace or (by implication) put to the blush: - confound, dishonour, (be a-, make a-) shame (-d).

Here is what you are to do with this thing called the Word of Faith according to Romans 10:9-10:
- Confess with your mouth Jesus as Lord.

CONFESS: homologeō (hom-ol-og-eh'-o)= to assent, that is, covenant, acknowledge: - con- (pro-) fess, confession is made, give thanks, promise.

Confessing is saying the same word as the Word of God, the Word of faith says. In this case you are confessing Jesus as Lord, Jesus as Kurios.

LORD: kurios (koo'-ree-os)=From kuros (supremacy); supreme in authority, that is, (as noun) controller; by implication Mr. (as a respectful title): - God, Lord, master, Sir.

When you confess Jesus as Kurios, you are saying that Jesus is in

control of my life. When you confess Jesus as Lord you are saying, "Yes, Lord."
- Believe in your heart that God has raised Him from the dead.

RAISED: egeirō (eg-i'-ro)= (through the idea of collecting one's faculties); to waken (transitively or intransitively), that is, rouse (literally from sleep, from sitting or lying, from disease, from death; or figuratively from obscurity, inactivity, ruins, nonexistence): - awake, lift (up), raise (again, up), rear up, (a-) rise (again, up), stand, take up.

This is also known as resurrection from the dead.
- With the heart a person believes resulting in righteousness

It is at this point we go from "none righteous no not one" (Romans 3:10) to "the righteous lives by faith" (Romans 1:17) as a result of being in Christ. (II Corinthians 5:21)

This is the heart of the matter with faith. When you believe you trust in, cling to, rely on and adhere to the Word (Jesus, God in the flesh) and The Word (the spoken and written revelation of God with (a) Logos (Low-goes) which is the universal Word (b) Rhema (ray-ma) which is the spoken personal Word. One is for the world, and the other is for you in the moment of need.
- With the mouth he confesses, resulting in salvation.

When you confess what you believe in your heart the cause and effect is salvation. Salvation is not just a ticket into heaven. It is the entrance point into the Kingdom of God that you walk by faith in the Kingdom (righteousness, peace and joy in the Holy Ghost, Romans 14:17) on earth as it is in heaven. (Matthew 6:10)

SALVATION: sōtēria (so-tay-ree'-ah)=Feminine of a derivative of G4990 as (properly abstract) noun; rescue or safety (physically or morally): - deliver, health, salvation, save, saving. G4990: sōtēr (so-tare')=From G4982; a deliverer, that is, God or Christ: - saviour. G4982: sōzō (sode'-zo)=From a primary word sōs (contraction for the obsolete saos, "safe"); to save, that is, deliver or protect (literally or figuratively): - heal, preserve, save (self), do well, be (make) whole.

I love the fact that this thing called *salvation* is not only your purchase of a ticket to heaven and you just sit in the station (pew in church) waiting for the Engineer to come back. As you walk and live by this thing called faith your will be living the maximized, overcoming, more than a conqueror, abundant, successful prosperous lifestyle that will touch every area of your life.

Once you enter into the Kingdom of God by being born again, you can now see the world differently, through Kingdom eyes. You are now moving through this world with a sense of righteousness (who you are in right standing with Him), peace (a wholeness and rest) and joy (not an emotional occurrence but a sense of well-being). You begin to walk in this world with authority (exousia, delegated authority) and power (dunamis, dynamic ability).

Without this thing that Jesus told us to have constantly (Mark 11:22 The Amplified Bible) we cannot please God.

PLEASE: euaresteō (yoo-ar-es-teh'-o)=From G2101; to gratify entirely: - please (well). G2101: euarestos (yoo-ar'-es-tos)= fully agreeable: - acceptable (-ted), wellpleasing.

While things may look impossible, in Christ, through God, by the Holy Spirit impossibilities can be turned into possibilities.

> *"But Jesus beheld them, and said unto them, with men this is impossible; but with God all things are possible."*
> ~Matthew 19:26, Mark 10:27

IMPOSSIBLE: adunatos (ad-oo'-nat-os)=; unable, that is, weak (literally or figuratively); passively impossible: - could not do, impossible, impotent, not possible, weak.

POSSIBLE: dunatos (doo-nat-os')=From G1410; powerful or capable (literally or figuratively); neuter possible: - able, could, (that is) mighty (man), possible, power, strong. G1410: dunamai (doo'-nam-ahee)=Of uncertain affinity; to be able or possible: - be able, can (do, + -not), could, may, might, be possible, be of power.

This word called possible is rooted in the word for power which is *duNAMis* which means dynamic ability.

POWER: dunamis (doo'-nam-is)=From G1410; force (literally or figuratively); specifically miraculous power (usually by implication a miracle itself): - ability, abundance, meaning, might (-ily, -y, -y deed), (worker of) miracle (-s), power, strength, violence, mighty (wonderful) work. G1410: dunamai (doo'-nam-ahee)=Of uncertain affinity; to be able or possible: - be able, can (do, + -not), could, may, might, *be possible*, be of power.

NOTE: I believe that what really pleases God is when we come to Him with impossible situations (outside our ability to handle it) and believe (trust in, cling to, rely on, adhere to) Jesus, who we acknowledge with our faith and actions that He is in control and will turn the impossible to possible.

According to Hebrews 11:6:
1. Without faith it is impossible to please Him
2. We must believe that He exists
3. We must come to Him believing (trusting in, clinging to, relying on, adhering to)
4. We must come to Him believing that He is a rewarder
5. We must diligently seek Him and not just passively inquire

Can you imagine how utilizing the principles outlined so far would affect your lifestyle and the outcome of everything that you do?

When you walk by faith and not by sight you will also talk by faith and not by sight. Abraham, the father of faith (Romans 4:16), is also known as Abraham the Believer (Galatians 3:9). This man, Abraham, exemplified how to speak in faith in Romans 4:16-21. This faith that He lived out loud was in accordance with grace and the promise given by God.

In Genesis 17:5 it stated, "A father of many nations have I made you…" (Romans 4:17, Genesis 17:5)

Abraham was also known as a believer.

*"…in the presence of Him (The Father God) whom he (Abraham)*

*believed, even God, who gives life to the dead and calls into being that which does not exist."*

~Romans 4:17 addition mine

*"…the God who gives life to the dead and calls into being things that were not."*

~Romans 4:17, NIV

*"believed in the God who brings the dead back to life and who creates new things out of nothing."*

~Romans 4:17, NLT

*"…he believed, who gives life to the dead and calls into existence the things that do not exist."*

~Romans 4:17, ESV

*"…in whom he believed, the God who gives life to the dead and calls into being what does not yet exist."*

~Romans 4:17, BSB

*"…whom he believed, the One giving life to the dead and calling into being the things not even existing."*

~Romans 4:17, BLB

*"…whom he believed, even God, who quickeneth the dead, and calleth those things which be not as though they were."*

~Romans 4:17, KJV

*"…believed—the God who gives life to the dead and calls things into existence that do not exist."*

~Romans 4:17, CSB

*"…he had faith in God, who raises the dead to life and creates new things."*

~Romans 4:17, CEV

> *"...believed—the God who brings the dead to life and whose command brings into being what did not exist."*
>
> ~Romans 4:17, GNT

> *"...who gives life to the dead and calls things into existence that do not exist."*
>
> ~Romans 4:17, HCSB

Thanx and a Tip O Da Hat to E-Sword for supplying various translations of section of Romans 4:17.

The bottom line is that Abraham believed God, and God spoke a certain way, and Abraham spoke and thought like God thought and spoke.

God calls things that are *not* as though they were while I find myself calling things that are not as if they will *never* change.

Abraham who had received a covenant promise from God at the young age of seventy-five and at the ripe old age of 100 years old had not yet received his promise—of a child and land.

> *"In hope against hope he believed, so that he might become a father of many nations according to that which had been spoke, so shall your descendants be."*
>
> ~Romans 4:18, Genesis 17:17, Genesis 18:11

Here is one of the key principles of success:

> *"...without becoming weak in faith , he contemplated his own body (did not take his body into consideration next to the promise), now as good as dead (unable to cause the promise to take place physically) since he was about a hundred years old, and the deadness of Sarah's womb (Abraham was shriveled and dried up and Sarah's womb was a tomb, unable to perform sexually to have children) yet, (in spite of) with respect to the promise of God (God's Word) , he did not waver in unbelief but grew strong in faith, giving glory to God, and being fully assured that what God had promised He was able to perform."*
>
> ~Romans 4:17-21 addition mine

When Abraham was not able to perform, God was able to perform.

Proponents of positive mental attitude (P.M.A.) believe in speaking forth a positive word versus a negative word. They believe in what we mentioned previously as The Law of Attraction, where how you speak, positively or negatively will attract positive and negative to you. They believe that you can have what you say. While I believe that the principle is true, the motivation is more humanistic than Godistic. They believe in "self-talk" which is a Biblical principle.

The Psalmist King David, wrote in Psalm 103:1-2 and told his own soul (mind, will, emotions, and the totality of who he was) to:
1. Bless the Lord, soul you bless the Lord
2. And all that is within me, including my spirit and my body, bless the Lord
3. Soul, don't forget any of God's benefits.

When King David was surrounded and being stoned because of his children, David encouraged himself.

> *"Moreover David was greatly distressed because the people spoke of stoning him, for all the people were embittered, each one because of his sons and his daughters. But David strengthened himself in the LORD his God."*
>
> ~I Samuel 30:6

So, what we think and what we say does make a difference in our attitude and our outcome.

As we come to the end of this chapter we have laid out a foundation for true P.M.A. (Positive Mental Attitude) under the Lordship of Jesus. If you are going to live the maximized, overcoming, more than conqueror, victorious, abundant, successful, prosperous lifestyle, what you believe will need to match up with how you speak and how you act.

# CHAPTER SEVEN

## THE SERVANT PRINCIPLE

SERVANT: diakonos (dee-ak'-on-os)=Probably from diakō to run on errands; an attendant, that is, (generally) a waiter (at table or in other menial duties); specifically a Christian teacher and pastor (technically a deacon or deaconess): - deacon, minister, servant.

When I am writing about the various principles found in this book, The Servant Principle is the #1 principle. To be great we must first must determine which Kingdom we want to be great within. There is a kingdom (little k) in this world where everyone is running in the rat race; where the winner of the rat race is the #1 rat. The obtaining and accumulation of stuff is the primary goal, and the primary mantra sounds like we are warming up to sing the praises of ourselves, "me, me, and me." If someone would asked what this life is all about, the respond would be, "It's all about me baby; all about me."

When our life is in the Kingdom of God, where our life is revolving around the throne of The King, we will develop the attitude of The King (Jesus).

KINGDOM: basileia (bas-il-i'-ah)=From G935; properly royalty, that is, (abstractly) rule, or (concretely) a realm (literally or figuratively): - kingdom, + reign G935: basileus (bas-il-yooce')=Probably from G939 (through the notion of a foundation of power); a sovereign (abstractly, relatively or figuratively): - king. G939: basis (bas'-ece)=From bainō (to walk); a pace ("base"), that is, (by implication) the foot: - foot.

The breakdown of a kingdom is:
1. Royalty
2. Rule
3. Realm
4. Reign
5. Foundation of Power
6. Sovereign
7. King
8. Basis
9. Walk
10. Pace
11. Foot

In karate, the foundation of a good kick, punch, or any technique is your stance. When you have proper placement of the foot, you can do what needs to be done. There is a stability in a good foundation of power. So it is with the Kingdom of God. Where the King rules, so can the subjects of the Kingdom serve not only the King but serve others, thus being great in the Kingdom of God.

NOTE: Throughout the Bible you will see the phrases, "Kingdom of God" and Kingdom of Heaven." I see the Kingdom of Heaven being the headquarters where the King's wish and desire is. The Kingdom of God is where the headquarters' will is manifested and revealed on earth. This manifestation was first seen in Jesus and was passed down to His followers back then and extends into His followers (us) now.

> *"At that time the disciples came to Jesus and said, "Who then is greatest in the kingdom of heaven?"*
>
> ~Matthew 18:1

GREATEST: meizōn (mide'-zone)= larger (literally or figuratively, specifically in age): - elder, greater (-est), more.

Jesus responded by bringing a child before them. The key to greatness is becoming *converted* like children. Without this principle you cannot enter the kingdom of heaven, much less be great in it.

CONVERTED: strephō (stref'-o)=Strengthened from the base of G5157; to twist, that is, turn quite around or reverse (literally or figuratively): - convert, turn (again, back again, self, self about). G5157: tropē (trop-ay')=From an apparently primary word trepō (to turn); a turn ("trope"), that is, revolution (figuratively variation): - turning.

Jesus told Nicodemus, a religious leader who came to Him at night (Nick at Night) that he must be born again (converted) if He wanted to see and enter the Kingdom of God. (John 3:3-8)

The # 1 key to being great is *humility*.

HUMBLE: tapeinoō (tap-i-no'-o)=From G5011; to depress; figuratively to humiliate (in condition or heart): - abase, bring low, humble (self). G5011: tapeinos (tap-i-nos')=Of uncertain derivation; depressed, that is, (figuratively) humiliated (in circumstances or disposition): - base, cast down, humble, of low degree (estate), lowly.

NOTE: Jesus was saying that a child is a picture of what it is like to be humble. That is confusing to me, because children—as tender and innocent as they are, especially as a baby—tend to be selfish and not serving. They tend to want what they want now, and if they don't get what they want as soon as they want it they will throw a fit. They will whine, cry, pout, and sulk if we don't serve them. I don't believe that is not what Jesus is talking about when he says, "Suffer the little children…" (Matthew 19:14) I don't believe that Jesus was talking about me suffering as the little tykes run roughshod over me. Of course, when Jesus said *suffer* he was talking about not preventing the children to come to Him.

The bottom line is that if you want to be great in God's Kingdom you will need to learn to be the servant of all.

> *"It is not this way among you, but whoever wishes to become great among you shall be your servant."*
> ~Matthew 20:26

Jesus gave the example of how to serve in Philippians 2:1-4.

*"Therefore if there is any encouragement in Christ, if there is any consolation of love, if there is any fellowship of the Spirit, if any affection and compassion, make my joy complete by being of the same mind, maintaining the same love, united in spirit, intent on one purpose. Do nothing from selfishness or empty conceit, but with humility of mind regard one another as more important than yourselves; do not merely look out for your own personal interests, but also for the interests of others."*
~Philippians 2:1-4

To be able to do this you will have to have what is known as an "attitudinal adjustment."

*"Have this attitude in yourselves which was also in Christ."*
~Philippians 2:5

MIND/ATTITUDE: phroneō (pron-eh'-o)=From G5424; to exercise the mind, that is, entertain or have a sentiment or opinion; by implication to be (mentally) disposed (more or less earnestly in a certain direction); intensively to interest oneself in (with concern or obedience): - set the affection on, (be) care (-ful), (be like-, + be of one, + be of the same, + let this) mind (-ed, regard, savour, think. G5424: phrēn (frane)= Probably from an obsolete phraō (to rein in or curb, the midriff (as a partition of the body), that is, (figuratively and by implication of sympathy) the feelings (or sensitive nature; by extension [also in the plural] the mind or cognitive faculties): - understanding.

An "attitudinal adjustment" is having a change of mind, heart, direction which is also known as repenting.

When you begin to start doing things not based on your empty conceit and start doing things based on "humility of mind" (how you thing about others), begin to:

*"...regard one another as more important than yourselves, do not merely look out for your own personal interest, but in contrast to*

*those things, begin to look out for the interests of others, then you will be able to be great in the Kingdom of God manifested here on earth.*
~Philippians 2:4

NOTE: I believe that if you want to be great in God's Kingdom you will be doing everything you can to help the other guy to become the greatest in the Kingdom rather than you.

# CHAPTER EIGHT

## THE HEALTHY ROOTS PRINCIPLE

We just finished the chapter on how to be great in God's Kingdom which in turn will produce greatness in your own life. The seeds that we plant in the soil of the Kingdom and in the soil of our lives will determine harvest in both areas. For this to take place there must be a healthy root system.

SEED: (1) the fertilized, matured ovule of a flowering plant, containing an embryo or rudimentary plant (2) any propagative part of a plant, including tubers, bulbs, etc., especially as preserved for growing a new crop.

SEED: zera (zeh'-rah)=From H2232; seed; figuratively fruit, plant, sowing time, posterity: - X carnally, child, fruitful, seed (-time), sowing-time. H2232: zâra (zaw-rah')=A primitive root; to sow; figuratively to disseminate, plant, fructify: - bear, conceive seed, set with, sow (-er), yield.

SOWED: speirō (spi'-ro)=Probably strengthened from G4685 (through the idea of extending); to scatter, that is, sow (literally or figuratively): - sow (-er), receive seed. G4685: spaō (spah'-o) =A primary verb; to draw: - draw (out).

For there to be a harvest (desired results) there must be
- A seed
- Soil
- A planting of the seed in the soil

- Cultivation of the seed
- Roots
- A time of growth
- Harvest.

Jesus teaches a parable in Mark chapter 4 on the process of soil, sowing, and the sower with the harvest (reward) being either no harvest because of attacks in the soil or various levels of success being thirty fold, sixty fold or one hundred fold. While Jesus was teaching a parable about seed, soil, and the sower, He was also teaching about roots that can either be sick or healthy and how to deal with soil so the seed could reach its maximum potential.

Jesus speaks of four types of soil:
1. Soil beside the road
2. Rocky soil
3. Soil with thorns
4. Good soil

## SOIL THEOLOGY

### 1. SOIL BESIDE THE ROAD

The seed was sown (broadcasted) and fell beside the road. The birds came and ate up the seed so there was no roots and no harvest. Jesus later on identifies the birds as satan/d-evil.

### 2. ROCKY SOIL

There was not much soil here because of the rocks. Immediately it sprang up because this soil had not depth. When the sun came out (had risen) what sprang up was scorched because of the heat of the sun. Because it had no root, it withered away. The rocky soil was identified as immediately receiving the seed but was temporary because of affliction or persecution arising because of the word. Not only was there immediate reception with joy, there was also an immediate falling away.

### 3. SOIL WITH THORNS

In this case the thorns (who had bad/evil roots) came up and choked out the seed and the cause and effect was it yielded no crop (harvest).

### 4. GOOD SOIL

The good soil defined in Luke 8:15.

1. Heard the Word
2. An honest and good heart
3. Held fast to the Word
4. Bore fruit with perseverance (never gave up).

## VINES, BRANCHES AND FRUIT (John 15:1–8)

Jesus was teaching again about bearing fruit He identifies Himself as the true vine and His Father is the vinedresser. (John 15:1) Jesus clarifies further the roles of the player with Jesus being the vine and us being the branches. (John 15:5) There is a process in the production/harvest of the fruit found in John 15:2–6.

1. The branch does not bear fruit.
2. The branch is pruned and taken away
3. When the branches are dried up they are gathered and cast into the fire and they are burned.

## THE FRUIT PRODUCTION (John 15:2–5)

Fruit productions includes:
1. No fruit
2. More fruit
3. Much fruit

The key to bearing more and much fruit physically in the vineyard and spiritual in God's vineyard is found in John 15:2-4.

1. Being pruned
2. Being taken away, tied up off the ground
3. Cleaning because of the word which Jesus has spoken
4. Abiding (continuing in the vine)

The bottom line is that apart from the vine nothing can happen.

> *"I (Jesus) am the vine and you (followers of Jesus) are the branches; he who abides (continues) in Me (Jesus) and I in him, he bears much fruit, for apart from Me (Jesus) you (insert your name here) can do nothing (zip, zilch, zero, nada)."*
>
> ~John 15:5 addition mine

## RECOMMENDED READING

Bruce Wilkinson, author of *The Prayer of Jabez,* also wrote a book called *The Secrets of The Vine (Breaking Through To Abundance).*

Success and maximum harvest (prosperity) is hinged on good roots. Dealing with the roots is part of the cultivation process.

CULTIVATE:
1. to prepare and work on (land) in order to raise crops
2. to promote or improve the growth of (a plant, crop, etc.) by labor and attention
3. to produce by culture
4. to develop or improve by education or training; train; refine
5. to promote the growth or development of (an art, science, etc.); foster.

~dictionary.com

When it looks like evildoers (doers of evil) and wrongdoers (doers of wrong) appear to be flourishing in the soil of life, the Psalmist tells us not to fret or be envious of them and their seemingly fruitful lives. If you go thorough Psalm 37 and circle the verbs and look at the cause and effect of doing the Word, you will see who is really successful and prosperous.

*"Trust in the Lord and do good; dwell in the land and cultivate faithfulness. Delight yourself in the Lord and He will give you the desires of your heart."*

~Psalm 37:4

1. Trust (believe in the Lord)
2. Do good (and not bad)
3. Dwell (take up residence and abide, continue)
4. Cultivate faithfulness (not only *your* faithfulness but feed on *His* faithfulness)
5. Delight yourself (become pliable to the Lord)
6. He (the Lord) will give you (plant into your fertile soil of) your heart desires (dreams, visions) and will not only plant them but will bring them to pass.

ROOT TREATMENT

*"The axe is already laid at the root of the trees; therefore every tree*

*that does not bear good fruit is cut down and thrown into the fire."*
~Matthew 3:10

This speaks of the Pharisees (not very fair you see) and the Sadducees (did not believe in the resurrection of the dead so they were sad you see). They were fruitless religious people and were not bearing fruit with repentance. The axe refers to Jesus being on the way to present a new and living way that would bear much fruit. (Matthew 3:1-13)

Money has gotten a bad rap over the years because of one verse:

*"Money is the root of all evil."*
~I Timothy 6:10

Of course this is one of the most misquoted verses in the Bible. The verse actually reads in reference to evil roots,

*"For the love of money is a root of all sorts of evil and by longing for it have wandered away from the faith and pierced themselves with many griefs."*
~I Timothy 6:10

LOVE OF MONEY: philarguria (fil-ar-goo-ree'-ah)=From G5366; avarice: - love of money. G5366: philarguros (fil-ar'-goo-ros)=fond of silver (money), that is avaricious (extreme greed for wealth or material gain): - covetous

NOTE: Money and things are the object of this lust.

ROOT: rhiza (hrid'-zah)= Apparently a primary word; a "root" (literally or figuratively): - root.

NOTE: The fruit (good or bad) is only as good as the seed and its root system.

EVIL: kakos (kak-os')=Apparently a primary word; worthless (intrinsically such; whereas G4190 properly refers to effects), that is, (subjectively) depraved, or (objectively) injurious: - bad, evil, harm, ill, noisome, wicked.

NOTE: One root can start all kinds (plural) of evil. Remember the d-evil is the root of evil and Jesus came for the purpose of destroying the works of the d-evil, turn him around to live-d. (I John 3:8)

LONGING/COVETING: oregomai (or-eg'-om-ahee)=Middle voice of apparently a prolonged form of an obsolete primary (compare G3735); to stretch oneself, that is, reach out after (long for): - covet after, desire.

NOTE: There is a big difference between love and lust. One fulfills and satisfies, while the other is continually seeking to be filled.

WANDERED AWAY/ERRED: apoplanaō ( ap-op-lan-ah'-oz)= to lead astray (figuratively); passively to stray (from truth): - err, seduce.

NOTE: There is nothing worse than being lost and going around in circles ending up nowhere.

FAITH: pistis (pis'-tis)= From G3982; persuasion, that is, credence; moral conviction (of religious truth, or the truthfulness of God or a religious teacher), especially reliance upon Christ for salvation; abstractly constancy in such profession; by extension the system of religious (Gospel) truth itself: - assurance, belief, believe, faith, fidelity. G3982: peithō (pi'-tho) =A primary verb; to convince (by argument, true or false); by analogy to pacify or conciliate (by other fair means); reflexively or passively to assent (to evidence or authority), to rely (by inward certainty): - agree, assure, believe, have confidence, be (wax) content, make friend, obey, persuade, trust, yield.

NOTE: Many without a faith in God have a faith in themselves and when they fail (as they will) they are left with nothing.

PIERCED THEMSELVES THROUGH: peripeirō

(per-ee-pi'-ro)= to penetrate entirely, that is, transfix (figuratively): - pierce through.

NOTE: This is self-destruction. Many in their quest for success and prosperity have ended up bringing themselves down.

## BITTER ROOTS

> *"See to it that no one comes short of the grace of God; that no root of bitterness springing up cause trouble, and by it, many will be defiled; that there be no immoral or godless person like Esau, who sold his own birthright for a single meal."*
> ~Hebrews 12:15-16

I like that phrase, "see to it." It speaks of personal responsibility for yourself and others.

1. No one comes short of the grace of God.
2. No root of bitterness springing up causing trouble
3. Many will be defiled
4. No immoral or godless person sell their birthright like Esau.

That root of bitterness grows all kinds of bad fruit and troubles if not dealt with.

# CHAPTER NINE

## THE MONEY, MONEY, MONEY PRINCIPLE

Many people measure success and prosperity by the size of their bank account, mutual funds, 401(k), and possessions. All of these things are represented by money.

MONEY: (1) any circulating medium of exchange, including coins, paper money, and demand deposits (2) paper money (3) gold, silver, or other metal in pieces of convenient form stamped by public authority and issued as a medium of exchange and measure of value. (4) any article or substance used as a medium of exchange, measure of wealth, or means of payment, as checks on demand deposit or cowrie. (dictionary.com)

MONEY: keseph (keh'-sef)=From H3700; silver (from its pale color); by implication money: - money, price, silver (-ling). H3700: kâsaph (kaw-saf)=A primitive root; properly to become pale, that is, (by implication) to pine after; also to fear: - [have] desire, be greedy, long, sore.

MONEY: argurion=ar-goo'-ree-on= silvery, that is, (by implication) cash; specifically a silverling (that is, drachma or shekel): - money, (piece of) silver (piece).

We saw in the previous chapter that it is not money that is *the root of all kinds of evil,* but *the love* (lust, avarice) *of money.*
We have seen that the love for this thing called money can have dire consequences in our lives. We see that this love/lust relationship

can be the "root of all kinds of evil," and that by longing for it with a deep desire many have wandered away from the faith and end up piercing themselves with many griefs. (I Timothy 6:10)

The symbol of success and prosperity in this age (and in other ages) has been *money*. Money and wealth (possessions) gets a bad rap, and people have been duped by the d-evil to believe that somehow their spirituality is based on their poverty. Many people point fingers at rich Christians and point their "Pharisee Phingers" at who they call people who believe a "prosperity Gospel." They skewer them in the media by cursing with words about their houses, cars, fill in the blank.

What they don't understand is that in their middle class mentality is that to people who live in 3rd world countries facing 3rd world poverty—they are the ones living in prosperity. While our brethren in the developing world have no TVs or cars, or fine and fancy houses; our typical contemporary Pharisees have four TVs, three cars parked in their concrete driveways, and a refrigerator filled with food in their large house with multiple square feet. They draw a regular paycheck which they deposit in an institution that houses their money, and fatten up their 401(k)s and their money market certificates, and when they go to the hospital when they are sick and rely on health insurance to pay for it.

Money is good, blessings and prosperity is good, yet the stuff we accumulate and the garages we put the stuff in is a problem many have. The same thing that is a blessing, can be a curse depending on your love relationship with them.

Many people declare that to be rich is wrong. Many people point a finger at those who are rich as being out of the "will of God" (and Rod), on earth as it is in heaven. Many lose their perspective when they forget who blessed others will riches.

> *"It is the blessing of the Lord that makes rich, and he adds no sorrow to it."*
>
> Proverbs 10:22

A good barometer of whether you have the love of money as your root system is if there is sorrow added to your riches.

Yes, there are many rich people who lose perspective. The truth is:

*"No man can serve two masters; for either he will hate the one and love the other, or he will be devoted to one and despise the other. You cannot serve God and mammon (wealth, money, riches)."*
~Luke 6:24 addition mine

MAMMON: mammōnas (mam-mo-nas')=Of Chaldee origin (confidence, that is, figuratively wealth, personified); mammonas, that is, avarice (deified): - mammon.

A song from *Grease* (the Broadway show and the movie) speaks about being devoted to the one you love, and that is so true.

When you love the Lord and you're devotion is to Him, then the despised thing (mammon/money) will be in the proper place.

The question is who gives us the power (ability) to gain wealth. Is it the d-evil or is it The Lord?

*"But you shall remember the LORD your God, for it is He who is giving you power to make wealth that He may confirm His covenant which He swore to your fathers, as it is this day."*
~Deuteronomy 8:18

The d-evil and you're flesh may twist the covenant of wealth, but God gives it to you. A good indication if you're money (mammon) has turned into bad roots and a despising of the Lord will be sorrow in your soul where your mind, will, and emotions are not renewed.

*"It is the blessing of the Lord that makes rich, And He adds no sorrow to it."*
~Pro-Verbs 10:22

Don't let/allow anyone speak of your blessings as being a curse!

To live the maximized, overcoming, more than a conqueror, abundant, successful, prosperous lifestyle you don't have to have money.

Many people live a very maximized, overcoming, more than conquer, abundant, successful, prosperous lifestyle without any money, money, money. But having money does not hurt.

In relationship to the Lord, prosperity, health, and our souls, John writes to Gaius his wish and desires for him in 3 John 2.

Some say this is just a greeting like, "Dear Gaius, I hope all is well..." but I think it is something that John really does want for him, and I think it is something that Jesus really wants for us also.

BELOVED: agapētos (ag-ap-ay-tos')=From G25; beloved: - (dearly, well) beloved, dear. G25: agapaō (ag-ap-ah'-o)= to love (in a social or moral sense): - (be-) love (-ed).

NOTE: This is not just some greeting to just anyone. This is a relation based on Jesus being Lord.

I PRAY: euchomai (yoo'-khom-ahee=Middle voice of a primary verb; to wish; by implication to pray to God: - pray, will, wish.

NOTE: I believe that this is a prayer and not just *Dear Gaius I hope all is well.* John is praying something, speaking something into his life, passing down a blessing.

ABOVE: peri (per-ee)= through (all over), that is, around; used in various applications, of place, cause or time the locality, circuit, matter, circumstance about, above, against, at, on behalf of, how it will go with, ([there-, where-]) of, on, over, pertaining (to), for sake, X (e-) state,

ALL THINGS: pas (pas)=Including all the forms of declension; apparently a primary word; all, any, every, the whole: - all (manner of, means) alway (-s), any (one), X daily, + ever, every (one, way), as many as, + no (-thing), X thoroughly, whatsoever, whole, whosoever.

NOTE: This includes all, every area of the life, above being the importance of his request, above everything else in his life.

THAT YOU MAY PROSPEROUS: uodoō (yoo-od-o'-o)= to help on the road, that is, (passively) succeed in reaching; figuratively to succeed in business affairs: - (have a) prosper (-ous journey).

NOTE: Success is not a bad thing. I believe that true success is accomplishing the purposes of God in your life. Success and Prosperity is hinged on our relation to the Word of God (see Joshua 1:8). This success that John is wishing is help on the road (of life), reaching the goal of success, accomplishing the will of God in business affairs (especially the business of the Kingdom) and to have a prosperous journey (the road towards the destination)

BE IN HEALTH: hugiainō (hoog-ee-ah'ee-no)=From G5199; to have sound health, that is, be well (in body); figuratively to be uncorrupt (true in doctrine): - be in health, (be safe and) sound, (be) whole (-some). G5119: hugiēs (hoog-ee-ace')=From the base of G837; healthy, that is, well (in body); figuratively true (in doctrine): - sound, whole. G5119: auxanō (owx-an'-o)=A prolonged form of a primary verb; to grow ("wax"), that is, enlarge (literally or figuratively, actively or passively): - grow (up), (give the) increase.

NOTE: Some believe that when it talks about health and healing that it means spiritual health and sin sickness, not physical sickness. Well, since sin is the root of death and sickness, dis-ease, dis-comfort, dys-function of our spiritual condition, I believe that the Scriptures bear out by watching Jesus for three years going about, doing good and healing *all* who were harrassed and oppressed by the d-evil under the anointing of the Father with the Holy Spirit and power (duNAmis, dynamic ability). (Acts 10:38)

EVEN AS: kathōs (kath-oce')=just (or inasmuch) as, that: - according to, (according, even) as, how, when.

NOTE: This speaks of the above physical wishes to be a mirror of the spiritual condition

SOUL PROSPERS: psuchē (psoo-khay')=From G5594; breath, that is, (by implication) spirit, abstractly or concretely (the animal sentient principle only; thus distinguished on the one hand from G4151, which is the rational and immortal soul; and on the other from G2222, which is mere vitality, even of plants: G4151: psuchē (psoo-khay')=From G5594; breath, that is, (by implication) spirit, abstractly or concretely (the animal sentient principle only; thus distinguished on the one hand from G4151, which is the rational and immortal soul; and on the other from G2222, which is mere vitality, even of plants: these terms thus exactly correspond respectively to the Hebrew [H5315], [H7307] and [H2416]: - heart (+ -ily), life, mind, soul, + us, + you. G5594: psuchō (psoo'-kho)=A primary verb; to breathe (voluntarily but gently; thus differing on the one hand from G4154, which denotes properly a forcible respiration; and on the other from the base of G109, which refers properly to an inanimate breeze), that is, (by implication of reduction of temperature by evaporation) to chill (figuratively): - wax cold.

In I Thessalonians 5:23 we see that we are a complex being comprised of spirit, soul, and body. It makes sense that God wants us to prosper in all three areas.

I believe that we live far below our potential to have the full vitality of His prosperity in our lives.

Be blessed (supremely happy to be envied by others) and highly favored by God and man (Pro-Verbs 3:1-8).

In our next chapter we will looks at The Secret Principle for our need and not our greed.

# CHAPTER TEN

## PRELUDE TO THE SECRET PRINCIPLE

A few years ago there was a book and a film out called *The Secret*. The premise was that there was a secret that very few knew, but those who knew the secret had tapped into the source of knowledge, wealth, power, and money. The secret was a principle that they called The Law of Attraction. It spoke of the power of speaking positive words which attracted what you spoke to yourself. This law worked in reverse also, if you speak negative words then you will attract negative things to you.

Napoleon Hill wrote *Think and Grow Rich*, *Outwitting the Devil* (d-evil, mine), *The Law of Success*, *Success Through a Positive Mental Attitude* (with W. Clement Stone), *Master Key to Success*, *Napoleon Hill's Keys to Success*, *How to Sell Your Way Through Life*, *You Can Work Your Own Miracles* and many, many more. He once famously said, *What the mind of man can conceive and believe, the mind of man can achieve.*

Napoleon Hill was influenced by primarily Andrew Carnegie—industrialist, business magnate, and philanthropist who encouraged the wealthy. According to various articles about Mr. Carnegie, he wrote an article called *The Gospel of Wealth*.

"*The Gospel of Wealth* called on the rich to use their wealth to improve society, and stimulated a wave of philanthropy." ~Wikipedia

As stated earlier, this book, *Living The Maximized Lifestyle*, was based on principles many positive thinkers teach and use. What separates other positive thinkers who use Positive Mental Attitude

(P.M.A.) is submitting these principles (laws) under the Lordship of Jesus. I also stated that these principles have roots in the Bible (The Word of God) and work for the Christian and the non-Christian alike.

"If Adolph Hitler says that the sky is blue, it is. Truth is truth. It is a true statement, no matter who says it." (Thanks to Edwin McKnight my brother in the Lord and our financial advisor).

So, the statements of the various industrialist, philosophers, and positive thinkers have the Word (laws and Biblical principles) in some of the statements, but so did the d-evil who quoted Scripture to Jesus in the wilderness of temptation.

NOTE: "Temptation is not necessarily designed to pull you into sin but to pull you away from who you are and your destiny." ~Larry Napier, Bible teacher

Jesus' response to the d-evil was,

> "...man shall not live by bread alone but by every Word that proceeds out of the mouth of God."
> 
> ~Matthew 4:5

Jesus is quoting the Old Testament to the d-evil, since Jesus was a good Jew. He quotes from the Pentateuch (the first five books of the Bible, attributed to Moses).

> "You shall remember all the way which the Lord your God has led you in the wilderness (same wilderness Jesus was in) these forty years, that He might humble you, testing you, to know what was in your heart whether you would keep His commandments or not. He humbled you and let/allowed you to be hungry, and fed you with manna which you did not know, nor did your fathers know, that He might make you understand that man does not live by bread alone, but man lives by everything that proceeds out of the mouth of the Lord."
> 
> ~Deuteronomy 8:2-3

NOTE: As a Speech-Language Pathologist I am excited about what is said in this verse.

> *"...but man lives by everything that proceeds out of the mouth of the Lord."*
>
> ~Deuteronomy 8:3

> *"...but by every Word that proceeds out of the mouth of God."*
>
> ~Matthew 4:5

Words are merely our thoughts that are expressed out of our mouth (or written or signed). In the natural the process of forming our thoughts into words is:
1. Think a thought
2. Take in a breath
3. Release a breath
4. Form words/thoughts with our articulators including the pharynx, tongue, teeth, lips, soft and hard palate. The words/thoughts are driven by breath.
5. Choose to speak those words.

In the spiritual realm:
1. Think thoughts with a renewed mind that is renewed by the Word of God
2. Take in a breath (the Holy Spirit)
3. Released a breath (the Holy Spirit exciting the body (our innermost being) like rivers of living water
4. Form God thoughts/Words with our articulators
5. Speak the Words that we live by and not just bread

We have been given the authority (exousa, delegated by God via Jesus to us) and the power (duNAmis, dynamic ability ) to speak Spirit driven Words. We speak God thoughts which God will honor.

Now, let us look at how anxiety can choke out the Word of God so we can't live a maximized, overcoming, more than a conqueror, abundant, successful and prosperous.

CHAPTER ELEVEN

## THE PEACE PRINCIPLE

Anxiety is a war that rages in a believer's heart and mind as well as the ones who are not believers in Jesus.

ANXIETY/ANXIOUS: merimnaō (mer-im-nah'-o)=From G3308; to be anxious about: - (be, have) care (-ful), take thought. G3308: merimna (mer'-im-nah)= From G3307 (through the idea of distraction); solicitude: - care. G3307: merizō (mer-id'-zo)= From G3313; to part, that is, (literally) to apportion, bestow, share, or (figuratively) to disunite, differ: - deal, be difference between, distribute, divide, give part. G3313: meros (mer'-os)=From an obsolete but more primary form of meiromai (to get as a section or allotment); a division or share (literally or figuratively, in a wide application): - behalf, coast, course, craft, particular (+ -ly), part (+ -ly), piece, portion, respect, side, some sort (-what).

SOLICITUDE: (1) The state of being solicitous; anxiety or concern. (2) Causes of anxiety or care (3) an attitude expressing excessive attentiveness

Has anyone said "take care" to you? Most likely they are just telling you to be careful as they show their concern for you. But if you look at the word solicitude, *taking care* takes on a whole new meaning. It says, "Take on anxiety or concern with an attitude expressing excessive attentiveness to the cares of this world." In my mind I immediately think, *I don't think so*. Back in 2107 when I had a (not *my*, I don't claim it) stroke, at rehab I was told that I was going to have a psychologist to come in to see me. When I told Brenda, she immediately said, "I don't receive what he has to say." She even came by the next day before the scheduled visit and anointed the door with oil as a symbol of the Holy Spirit that he had to pass through.

Well, he showed up and tried to convince me that I was depressed, which I was not. The Holy Spirit instructed me not to argue with him and to not receive his words. He came back one more time, and the first words he said were, "Well Mr. Boyd I see you are still depressed." This time the Holy Spirit told me I could speak to him. I got real close to his face and said, "Are you depressed because I am not depressed? He hemmed and hawed and left and never came back.

I had a peace that surpassed all understanding while all around me swirled a reason to be anxious.

PEACE: eirēnē (i-rah'-nay)=Probably from a primary verb eirō (to join); peace (literally or figuratively); by implication prosperity: - one, peace, quietness, rest, + set at one again.

Philippians 4:1-3 speaks of what we are to do to set ourselves into position not to be anxious.
1. Stand firm in the Lord
2. Live in harmony
3. Help those who are not in harmony
4. Rejoice in the Lord always
5. Let/Allow your gentle spirit be known to all men
6. Realize the Lord is near

## HOW TO DEAL WITH ANXIETY

*"Be anxious (don't be anxious) for nothing (no thing, zip, zilch, zero, nada) BUT (in contrast to being anxious) in everything (in the good, the bad and the ugly) by prayer and supplication with thanksgiving let your request be mad know to God."*
~Philippians 4:6

EXERCISE: Take a sheet of paper and draw a line down the middle.

On one side of the line write NOTHING and on the other side write EVERYTHING. Now on the NOTHING side, list everything you are anxious about. The draw an arrow to the EVERYTHING side, realizing that all your NOTHINGS are the same things you are not to be anxious about. Then begin to pray (talk to God about what you are anxious about) and supplicate (be humbly specific about your prayers) and then begin to give thanks to God (thanksgiving)—not for your problems but in spite of them. Choose to thank Him for meeting all your needs according to His riches in glory and in Christ Jesus (more on that later).

The cause and effect of you doing these things is, the peace (wholeness, rest, being brought back to one again instead of being pulled in 20 different directions with anxiety), that surpasses all comprehension (peace while what caused the anxiety may still be there) will guard (protect) you heart and your mind (the battlefield) in Christ Jesus. Outside of Christ Jesus there is anxiety, worry, tension, fear, doubt unbelief.

## HOW CAN YOU GUARD YOU HEART AND MIND?

Philippians 4:8 tells us to think on whatever is:
1. True
2. Honorable
3. Right
4. Pure
5. Lovely
6. Good Report
7. Any excellence
8. Anything worthy of praise.

We are to let/allow our minds to dwell on these things.

Various positive thinkers around this world encourage their followers to find someone who can mentor them. They look for someone to speak positive thoughts into their lives. If we are going to live a maximized, overcoming, more than conqueror, abundant, prosperous, successful lifestyle, we will need to find someone that we can trust who is living out the things that we are to allowing our mind to dwell upon.

Philippians 4:9, Paul tells us that we should practice the things we have:
1. Learned
2. Received
3. Heard
4. Seen in him

The cause and effect will be the God of peace (not the God of anxiety) will be with you.

Now we are ready to learn The Secret Principle

# CHAPTER TWELVE

## THE SECRET PRINCIPLE

As stated in Chapter 6, *The Prelude To The Secret Principle*, there was a book and movie called *The Secret* that identified the secret as a law/principle called The Law of Attraction that is elicited by what we speak—positive or negative—that will attract those things to us and affect our lives. I don't object to this Law of Attraction. We take laws and principles of things like the Law of Gravity. I think that the Law of Attraction is a Biblical Principle. We will cover this more in depth in a chapter called *The Calling Principle* that will deal with our words.

Paul was writing the book (epistle/letter) of Philippians from a jail cell/dungeon. Did you know that you can live a maximized, overcoming, more than a conqueror, abundant, successful, prosperous lifestyle in a prison? (See Acts 16:16-40) The bottom line is that Paul was imprisoned again for preaching the Gospel of Christ. While he was shackled by a heavy burden (a tip of the hat to Bill Gaither's beloved song, "He Touched Me"), Paul and his companion, Silas, were bent over in a cell with a low ceiling. Instead of grumbling and complaining about his current situation, they began singing praises unto God.

> *"But about midnight (in the midnight hour) Paul and Silas were praying and singing hymns of praise to God, and the prisoners were listening to them (people are watching and listening to you and how you respond to trials, troubles, and tribulations); and suddenly (the things of God can go from bad to good in the wink of an eye) there came a great earthquake, so that the foundations*

*of the prison house were shaken (all shook up); and immediately all the doors were opened and everyone's chains (not just Paul and Silas') were unfastened.*

~Acts 16:26 addition mine

NOTE: This version of the song "Jailhouse Rock" was being sung way before 1957 when Elvis recorded his hit song of the same title)..

Paul was using The Law of Attraction—or The Praise Principle—to attract what he needed. The overflow of the blessings was that the jailer was diverted from suicide to the jailer and his whole family was saved. The cause and effect of The Praise Principle (the Law of Attraction) was that deliverance was attracted and came Paul and Silas' way.

Paul was in financial need, and he was rejoicing in the Lord greatly (not just mediocre rejoicing). The people were concerned before, but now there was a shift in opportunity. They lacked opportunity, and now an opportunity appeared.

Now we are beginning to tap into The Secret.

*"Not that I speak from want for I have learned to be content in whatever circumstances I am."*

~Philippians 4:11

The principles of God are not received by osmosis but by trial and error; they are learned.

LEARNED: manthanō (man-than'-o)= to learn (in any way): - learn, understand.

Paul had to learn how to speak from a position of contentment.

SPEAK: legō (leg'-o)=A primary verb; properly to "lay" forth, that is, (figuratively) relate (in words [usually of systematic or set discourse; whereas G2036 and G5346 generally refer to an individual expression or speech respectively; while G4483 is properly to break silence merely, and G2980 means an extended or random harangue]); by implication to mean: - ask, bid, boast, call, describe, give out, name, put forth, say (-ing, on), shew, speak, tell, utter.

Paul's speaking was positional. Paul had learned not to speak from a position of want.

WANT: husterēsis (hoos-ter'-ay-sis)=From G5302; a falling short, that is, (specifically) penury: - want. G5302: hustereō (hoos-ter-eh'-o)=From G5306; to be later, that is, (by implication) to be inferior; genitively to fall short (be deficient): - come behind (short), be destitute, fall, lack, suffer need, (be in) want, be the worse.

Paul's wants were real. They were a reality, but Paul guarded his speech and did not speak from what he did not have, but he had learned The Secret.
Me, I tend to mouth off about what I need and want, and when I don't get it, I begin to complain about what I don't have. Yes, I believe that as long as I speak that way, I will attract the exact opposite of what I want and need.
What had Paul learned?

*"Not that I speak from want...."*
~Philippians 4:11

*"I have learned to be content."*
~Philippians 4:11

CONTENT: autarkēs (ow-tar'-kace)= self-complacent, that is, contented: - content.

Where did Paul's contentment lay? (Philippians 4:11)

WHATSOEVER STATE/CIRCUMSTANCE: hos hē ho (hos, hay, ho)=Probably a primary word (or perhaps a form of the article G3588 the relative (sometimes demonstrative) pronoun, who, which, what, that: - one, (an-, the) other, some, that, what, which, who (-m,

-se), etc.: hou (hoo) at which place, that is, where: - where (-in), whither ([-soever]).

NOTE: Whatsoever state/circumstance can be when he/you are in prison or when he/you are out of prison. (Fill in whatever situation and circumstance that you are in right now, and learn how to speak in there). For Paul, speaking was praising, the language of the Lord. It has been said that grumbling and complaining is nothing but d-evil praise. Whatever you speak will be.

Paul, as he had learned The Secret, came to a knowledge where he knew how to do something.

"I know how to get along with humble means, and I also know how to live in prosperity…"

Many have learned that part about living in humble means (not being rich) but have a problem with prosperity.

PROSPERITY/ABOUND: perisseuō (per-is-syoo'-o)=From G4053; to superabound (in quantity or quality), be in excess, be superfluous; also (transitively) to cause to superabound or excel: - (make, more) abound, (have, have more) abundance, (be more) abundant, be the better, enough and to spare, exceed, excel, increase, be left, redound, remain (over and above). G4053: perissos (per-is-sos')= (in the sense of beyond); superabundant (in quantity) or superior (in quality); by implication excessive; adverb (with G1537) violently; neuter (as noun) preeminence: - exceeding abundantly above, more abundantly, advantage, exceedingly, very highly, beyond measure, more, superfluous, vehement [-ly].

John when he was writing to Gaius (the elder), who he loved in the truth, wished and prayed that,

> "…*in all respects you may prosper and be in good health, just as your soul prospers."*
>
> ~3rd John 2

Those who are anti-prosperity and pro-poverty, tell us that what

John was really doing was starting off a letter/salutation and not really wanting Gaius to prosper or even be in health like his mind, will and emotions was prospering.

Paul had learned The Secret relating to money.

> *"...in any and every circumstance I have learned The Secret of being filled (prosperous) and going hungry (not prosperous) both of having abundance (a lot of stuff) and suffering need (not having a lot of stuff).*
> ~Philippians 4:12 addition mine

Paul then states a mindblower in relationship to finances.

> *I can do all things (having and not having) through Him (Jesus) who strengthens me (in whatever state I am in).*
> ~Philippians 4:13 addition mine

# CHAPTER THIRTEEN

## THE THINKING IMAGINATION SPEAKING PRINCIPLE

Remember *The Secret* book and movie that we have talked about? Do you remember what The Secret was? Let me refresh your memory, The Secret was what is known as the Law of Attraction. A law is a principle that works for everyone. For example the Law of Gravity works on every one of the current seven billion plus people on planet Earth and all of the previous inhabitants from "in the beginning" (Genesis 1:1). The Law of Attraction, in a nutshell, states that what you think and speak (positive or negative thoughts and words) will be attracted to you. I believe it.

Have you ever notice someone who sounds like Eyore (of Winnie the Pooh books and cartoons/movies fame)?

EYORE: (1) Anyone who goes through life moping around with a poor me attitude. (2) The actual act of moping and complaining repeatedly, or just being depressed. (urbandictionary.com)

Eyore always looks at the negative and moans and groans about everything. Do you know people like Eyore? There is always something bad happening to them. They are hopeless as opposed to being full of hope.

Hope means to have confident expectation while hopeless people are confident that bad stuff will happen.

In the charismatic movement, the belief that the Holy Spirit and His gifts are still alive and well spawned what is known at The Word of Faith movement within the church. To some this a corruption of Christianity while others believe it is "the full Gospel." The bad rap for these people that they believe in "name it and claim it." Some may misuse the principles of God as tools of manipulation to get what they want, like "writing your check to God."

I believe that many throw out the baby with the bath water and swing the opposite way away from proponents of The Law of Attraction to the point of disallowing any of the shenanigans of P.M.A. (Positive Mental Attitude) or Charismatic mumbo jumbo.

*"Unrestrained thoughts (what we think) produces unrestrained words (what we say) resulting in unrestrained actions (what we do)."*

~Kenneth Copeland
*How to Discipline the Flesh* addition mine

God is the first one who had a thought and expressed His thoughts out loud.

*"Then God said, "let there be light;" and there was light."*
~Genesis 1:3

God then declared whether or not if His thoughts and Words were negative or positive when He said:

*"God saw that the light was good (not bad or negative)."*
~Genesis 1:4 addition mine

In the creative process God in Genesis 1:1-31:
1. Said
2. Saw
3. Separated
4. Called
5. Made
6. Placed
7. Created
8. Blessed
9. Gave
10. Let

Throughout the creative process by the Creator, God positively affirmed creation by using phrases like, "it was good" and "very good'.

> "God saw all that He had made, and behold, it was very good…"
> ~Genesis 1:31

Man and Wo-man, through which all mankind was propagated, were from the imagination and blueprint of God out of a business meeting between the Father, the Son, and the Holy Ghost. Of course this is my imagination about the creative process.

> "Then God said, let Us make man in our image, according to Our likeness and let them rule over the fish of the sea and over the birds of the sky and over the cattle and over all the earth, and over every creeping thing that creeps on earth."
> ~Genesis 1:26

NOTE: Some theologians have speculated that the "Us" and "Our" in this verse was talking about angelic beings. In my humble opinion, the theologians are wrong. I can speculate just as good as they can. You can form your own opinion, angels versus the Father, Son and Holy Ghost. I see:

1. God: Chief Executive Officer (CEO)
2. Jesus: Chief Financial Officer (CFO)
3. The Holy Spirit: Chief Operating Officer (COO)
4. The image and likeness: The blueprint
5. Them: man (Adam) and female (Eve), the created expression of God's thoughts
6. Blessed: The will of God on Earth as it is in Heaven
7. Subdue and Rule: Dominion over every living thing including every creeping thing that creeps on the earth.

NOTE: Adam and Eve had dominion/rule/and subduing authority over everything that creeps on earth—including the serpent/satan. My speculation is that their authority was in the words that they spoke that lined up with the thoughts and Words of God.

There was a time in earth history that the whole earth used the same language and the same words. As a Speech-Language Pathologist I find this passage in Genesis 11:1-9 to be very interesting.

## THE LANGUAGE OF IMAGINATION

LANGUAGE: śâphâh śepheth (saw-faw', sef-eth')=) the lip (as a natural boundary); by implication language; by analogy a margin (of a vessel, water, cloth, etc.): - band, bank, binding, border, brim, brink, edge, language, lip, prating, ([sea-]) shore, side, speech, talk, [vain] words.

LANGUAGE: Any accepted, structured, symbolic system for interpersonal communication composed of sounds arrange in ordered sequence s or strings that express thoughts, intentions, experiences, and feelings. Composed of phonological (sounds), morphological (simplest form of sounds), syntactical (word order) and semantical (word meaning) components. ("Terminology of Communication Disorders," *Speech-Language-Hearing*), Nicolosi, Harryman and Kresheck)

WORDS: dâbâr (daw-bawr')= a word; by implication a matter (as spoken of) of thing; adverbially a cause: - act, advice, affair, answer, X any such (thing), + because of, book, business, care, case, cause, certain rate, + chronicles, commandment, X commune (-ication), + concern [-ing], + confer, counsel, + dearth, decree, deed, X disease, due, duty, effect, + eloquent, errand, [evil favoured-] ness, + glory, + harm, hurt, + iniquity, + judgment, language, + lying, manner, matter, message, [no] thing, oracle, X ought, X parts, + pertaining, + please, portion, + power, promise, provision, purpose, question, rate, reason, report, request, X (as hast) said, sake, saying, sentence, + sign, + so, some [uncleanness], somewhat to say, + song, speech, X spoken, talk, task, + that, X there done, thing (concerning), thought, + thus, tidings, what [-soever], + wherewith, which, word, work.

WORD: Free form consisting of a sequence of one or more phonemes and one or more syllables which have meaning without being divisible into smaller units capable of independent use. (*Speech-Language-Hearing*, Nicolosi, Harryman and Kresheck)

So here are the Shinarites (in the land of Shinar) settling in and speaking the language of Shinar. They were conversing in their language (an agreed upon code) and suggested that they make bricks and burn them thoroughly. They would be man-made bricks (with tar) versus God-made stones (mortar). That should have been the first clue that something was amiss. (Genesis 11:3)

Continuing with the dialogue they suggested that they (together [us]) should build for themselves (not for God) a city and a tower. In my imagination, I see a bustling city with a tower rising smack dab out of the middle of the city. This was the suggestion of the first skyscraper that would reach to the heaven. The purpose for the city and tower was not for God but so that they could make a name for themselves. There reasoning (logical thinking) was that they would be scattered abroad over the face of the whole earth without a city and a tower. (Genesis 11:3-4)

The Lord came down to Shinar to check things out to see the city and the tower that the sons of men had built. (Genesis 11:6)

*"And the LORD said, Behold, the people is one, and they have all one language; and this they begin to do: and now nothing will be restrained from them, which they have imagined to do."*
*~Genesis 11:6 (KJV)*

IMAGINATION: zâmam (zaw-mam')=A primitive root; to plan, usually in a bad sense: - consider, devise, imagine, plot, purpose, think (evil).

NOTE: Not all imagination is bad, but when it excludes God from the mix and focuses on human beings, it is bad. God appears to have an imagination about what He desired with the creation of the world and mankind. Through disobedience in the Garden, God's imagination was corrupted. As stated previously, Positive Mental (imagination) Attitude (P.M.A.) without God as the center of the imagination is humanism where the humans become their own God. Nothing (zip, zilch, zero, nada, nothing) that they imagined with their minds would be impossible.

IMPOSSIBLE/RESTRAIN: bâtsar (baw-tsar')=A primitive root; to clip off; to gather grapes; also to be isolated (that is, inaccessible by height or fortification): - cut off, (de-) fenced, fortify, (grape) gather (-er), mighty things, restrain, strong, wall (up), withhold.

> *"Where there is no vision, the people perish: but he that keepeth the law, happy is he."*
> ~Pro-Verbs 29:18 (KJV)

> *"Where there is no vision, the people are unrestrained, But happy is he who keeps the law."*
> ~Pro-Verbs 29:18 (NASB)

> *"Where there is no vison [no redemptive revelation of God], the people perish; but he who keeps the law [of God], which includes that of man]—blessed (happy, fortunate, and enviable) is he."*
> ~Pro-Verbs 29:18 (AMP)

> *"Without a fresh revelatory prophetic word from the Lord, my people are destroyed or consumed."*
> ~Pro-Verbs 29:18 (Kirk DeVinney personal translation)

Without a God's eyed-view of things, without a revelatory imagination and vision, the people will be unrestrained, just doing what they will do, and the end will be destruction.

NOTE: How we think will be how we speak and will be how we do.

The cause and effect of speaking their own language was that the Lord and "Us" (same us in Genesis 1:26) confused their language that they may not understand one another's speech. The Lord then scattered; exactly what the Shinarites were trying to stop from happening by building a city, tower and name for themselves. The city was given the name of Babel (not *Babble*, but *bAbel*) because there the Lord confused the language of the whole earth; and from there the Lord scattered them abroad over the face of the earth. (Genesis 11:7-9)

We have mentioned previously in this chapter, "Unrestrained thought (what we think) results in unrestrained words (what we say) resulting in unrestrained actions (what we do)."

We restrain ourselves by renewing our minds with the Word of God (God thoughts) and speak out those thoughts to ourselves, others, and to the mountains and obstacles and the d-evil. We have God-given authority to speak this way (authority, exousia, delegated power) and can expect our words to have power behind them (power, duNAmis, delegated authority).

If our imaginations are not renewed based on the Word of God with our minds set (mindset) on the Spirit, we will be having our minds set (mindset) on the flesh.

> *"...us who walk not according to the flesh but according to the Spirit. For those who are according to the flesh set their minds (mindset) on the things of the flesh, but those who are according to the Spirit, the things of the Spirit. For the mind set on the flesh is death, but the mind set on the Spirit is life and peace, because the mind set on the flesh is hostile toward God; for it does not subject itself to the law (principles) of God, for it is not even able to do so, and those who are in the flesh cannot please God."*
>
> ~Romans 8:4-8

With a revelatory vision there will be no revelatory imagination. This type of thinking, speaking (with the same language) and doing, an individual will never live the maximized, overcoming, more than conqueror, abundant, blessed, successful, prosperous lifestyle.

CHAPTER FOURTEEN

## THE TITHE/GIVING PRINCIPLE (RECIPROCITY) PRINCIPLE

One of the hallmarks of successful people is their willingness to give away their wealth. The saying is, "You can't out give God." Another saying is, If you are in financial difficulty, you need to give your way out of it."

Andrew Carnegie who was an industrialist, philosopher, and a very wealthy man who influenced and encouraged Napoleon Hill to study the principles of success and then write his first book, *Think and Grow Rich*. He wrote an article about what to do with your wealth. It appears that many wealthy people—from inventors to entrepreneurs—learned what The Secret of the Law of Attraction was. They not only thought and spoke positive things, but their actions of giving away money was also seen in them. His 1889 article proclaiming "The Gospel of Wealth" called on the rich to use their wealth to improve society, and stimulated a wave of philanthropy.

In 1982 Pat Robertson and Bob Slosser wrote a book entitled *The Secret Kingdom* about how this visible, physical world was undergirded by an invisible, secret world called the Kingdom of God. The book covers laws and principles of the Kingdom of God with one of them being The Law of Reciprocity.

As we have stated many times throughout this book, natural physical laws and principles work. They are real for anyone who chooses to submit to them and learn how to work them. For example, for every action there is an equal and opposite reaction. There is a Law of Gravity that when combined with the law of thrust and lift, the equal and opposite reaction gives us the ability to fly in the air in airplanes, jets, and helicopters.

The law of reciprocity is seen all throughout the Bible.

The Golden Rule (also found in many other religions) states;

> *"Do unto others (treat them) as you would have them do unto you (treat you).*
> 
> ~Luke 6:31 addition mine

This principle or law is found in Jesus' teaching about how the Kingdom of God operates. As Bob Mumford teaches in his book, *The King and You,* how the Sermon on the Mount (Matthew 5:17-48 gives the framework for the Constitution of the Kingdom of God.

Some call this sermon the foundation of blessings in our lives.

BLESSED: Makarios (mak-ar'-ee-os)=A prolonged form of the poetical makar (meaning the same); supremely blest; by extension fortunate, well off: - blessed, happy (X -ier).

TITHE: mah-as-ar', mah-as-raw')= a tenth; especially a tithe: - tenth (part), tithe (-ing).

This principle of tithing is definitely an Old Testament Principle, but it was not a principle that started with the Law. Tithing was prior to the giving of the Law of Moses and was still intact during the days of Jesus. Jesus spoke about tithing, not condemning the practice but encouraging to tithe for the proper reasons.

> *"Woe to you, scribes and Pharisees, hypocrites! For you tithe mint and dill and cumin, and have neglected the weightier provisions of the law: justice and mercy and faithfulness; but these are the things you should have done without neglecting the others."*
> 
> ~Mathew 23:23

The religious people, the scribes and the Pharisees, tithed but with the wrong motive. They neglected the "weightier" (more important) things of the Law (although tithing was not instituted with the law). The weightier things including justice, mercy, and faithfulness.

> *"He hath shewed thee, O man, what is good; and what doth the LORD require of thee, but to do justly, and to love mercy, and to walk humbly with thy God?"*
>
> ~Micah 6:8

Jesus always directed them back to the Old Testament writings. When asked what was the greatest commandment, He referred back to the Shema (Leviticus 19:18, Deuteronomy 3:25, Deuteronomy 6:5, James 2:19)

> *"Jesus answered, "The foremost (commandment) is 'Hear, O Israel! The Lord our God is one Lord; and you shall love the Lord your god with all your heart, and with all your soul, and with all your mind, and with all your strength!' The second command is this, 'You shall love your neighbor as yourself.' There is no other commandment greater than these."*
>
> ~Mark 12:29-31

If all the other commands of the Law and even the pre-Law were not filtered through love of the One God, then you were a Pharisee. Some still are to this day as we debate, quibble, and nitpick Scripture.

The first reference to tithing is found in Genesis 14:18.

> *"And Melchizedek king of Salem (old Jerusalem, city of peace) brought out bread and wine; now he was a priest of God Most High. He blessed him and said, "Blessed be Abram of God Most High, possessor of heaven and hearth ; and blessed be God Most High, Who has delivered your enemies into your hand." He (Melchizedek the king/priest) gave him a tenth of all."*
>
> Genesis 14:19-20

NOTE: I see a few things here:

1. This king was also a priest.
2. Salem was Jerusalem the city of peace
3. The king/priest brought out to Abram who had just won a victory over the kings of Sodom and Gomorrah
4. The king/priest blessed the covenant warrior (Abram soon to be Abraham the Believer)
5. The king/priest acknowledge the victory of Abram
6. The king/priest acknowledged the One God as possessor or heaven and earth.
7. The king/priest gave (of his own free will) a tenth/tithe of all (the bread and wine)

NOTE: Melchizedek did not *take* the tithe, it was *given* willingly. Today in church there comes a time in the service where someone says, "It is time to take the offering." No, it is time for you, the people of the church to "give the offering."

NOTE TO THE NOTE: In the church today, prior to "taking the offering" we have respected men and women of the local body to get up and encourage us to give our tithes and offerings. Some may feel like the church is just trying to get your money or trying to manipulate you. Even the men and women of God who are feeding the sheep feel guilty about the process. I say no, they are merely trying to reach us again what tithing and giving is all about. I like what Paul said about his teachings.

> *"Finally, my brethren, rejoice in the Lord. To write the same things again is no trouble to me, and it is a safeguard for you."*
> Philippians 3:1

In the Old Testament they did not have to be manipulate and cajoled into giving the tithe of their money and stuff.

> *"Then it shall be, when you enter the land (of promise) which the Lord your god gives you, and you shall put it (the tithe/first fruits) in a basket and go to the place where the Lord your God chooses to establish His name."*
> Deuteronomy 26:1-2 addition mine

NOTE: Excuse me while I express myself—*Oh glory to God, Hal-le-lu-ya!*

Notice in this verse:
1. They knew what they needed to do. At one point they were taught and it became the natural response. We, especially Americans in the Western world need to be reminded and taught again.
2. The land of promise (aka The Promised Land) was very fruitful but there would be battles to possess the land.
3. The land was not only promised but the land was given.
4. The first fruits/tithes were collected to be brought. It was a thought out process before entering the established place. In our day and age the established place was the local church where you are fed and taught.
5. This place was established by His name which happens to be Jehovah Jireh (the provider or the one who reveals the provision, like the Lord showing Abraham the sacrifice in place of Isaac. Jesus is the revealed provision for sacrifice in our place. Jesus is the revealed propitiation (satisfactory substitute).

*"You shall go to the priest who is in office at that time and say to him, 'I declare this day to the Lord my God that I have entered the land which the Lord swore to our fathers to give us.' Then the priest shall take the basket (filled with the tithe and first fruits) from your hand (they only took as they gave) and set it down before the altar of the Lord Your God."*
~Deuteronomy 26:3-4 addition mine

1. They went to the priest (today our pastors) and made a declaration of faith about the tithe/offering they were bringing.
2. The priest then took the basket from their hands. Again, to take it has to be given first.
3. The basket filled with the tithe/first fruits was set down before the altar of the Lord.

## THE MALACHI CONNECTION (Malachi 3:7-12)
The first word on tithing in the Old Testament was found in

Genesis 14:18 and the last word on tithing in the Old Testament is found in the Book of Malachi.

Back in the day the children of Israel had turned aside from God, again. They had turned away from God by turning away from his statues by not keeping them. God pleads for them to return to Him with the promise that He would return to them. God poses the question about what they might say;

*"How shall we return?"*

~Malachi 3:7

God answers His own question with the answer;

*"Will a man rob God?"*

The answer about their turning and their return is rooted in tithes and offerings.

*"Yet you are robbing Me! But you say, how have we robbed You?"* God clarifies, *"In tithes and offerings."*

~Malachi 3:8

It appears that this robbery of God, opened the door to a curse.

*"You are cursed with a curse, for you are robbing Me (God), the whole nation of you."*

~Malachi 3:9 addition mine

Now the question is, how can they return to God and remove the curse that they opened up for themselves?

*"Bring the whole tithe into the storehouse, so that there may be food in my house…"*

~Malachi 3:9

When they repent, turn, and bring back into the storehouse what they have withheld by withholding and robbing God, they in essence are reversing the curse—including a financial curse.

When they do this, they are testing the Lord. They are not tempting (testing) the Lord, but at His invitation they will test the Lord to see if He will do (and He does) what He says He will do.

> *"...and test Me now in this (the tithing principle), says the Lord of hosts, if I will not open for you the windows of heaven and pour out for you a blessing until it overflows."*
> ~Malachi 3:10

There was a chorus we use to sing back in the '70s called "The Windows of Heaven" which conveyed the thoughts that there were windows in heaven, and they were open. Out of opened windows of heaven there were blessings flowing. The cause and effect of flowing blessings was joy, joy, and joy. The joy resided in the hearts. Why? Because Jesus made everything right. When we exchanged our old tattered garments (giving), the return was a robe of pure white (receiving) as we feasted on manna from heaven which reflected that I was happy tonight (and in the daytime also).

Not only did (and does) the blessings flow, the Lord also will rebuke the devourer for us, so that the devourer will not destroy the fruits of the ground (the harvest from sowing and reaping, giving) so the field will not cast its grapes (which are our by right).

One of the meanings for being blessed is to be supremely happy and to be envied by others who see what you've got and want what you've got. This is how this section ends in Malachi.

> *"All the nations will call you blessed, for you shall be a delightful land, says the Lord."*
> ~Malachi 3:12

NOTE: This thing called tithing is an act of worship to God. When the men and women of God are teaching (again) about tithing/giving, they are merely teaching us about worship of the Most High God.

NOTE: When I say *Hallelujah* I ain't just quietly and reverently giving praise for these revelations of the Word of God concerning tithing. Here is what I am doing.

PRAISE: hâlal (haw-lal')=A primitive root; to be clear (originally of sound, but usually of color); to shine; hence to make a show; to boast; and thus to be (clamorously) foolish; to rave; causatively to celebrate; also to stultify: - (make) boast (self), celebrate, commend, (deal, make), fool (-ish, -ly), glory, give [light], be (make, feign self) mad (against), give in marriage, [sing, be worthy of] praise, rage, renowned, shine.

1. To be clear (no doubt about what I mean when I praise Him)
2. Clear in the sense of sound and color
3. To make a show
4. To boast
5. To be clamorously foolish (I am a fool for Christ, tell me whose fool you are)
6. To celebrate (let's have a party)
7. To Commend (commend and recommend)
8. To feign (fake) madness
9. To rave (like a lunatic)
10. To shine.

> "Now behold, I have brought the first (tithe/first fruits, off the top of my paycheck) of the ground (this earthly place of employment) which You, O Lord have given me.' (Stop griping about your job). And you shall set it down before the Lord your God and worship before the Lord your God."
> ~Deuteronomy 26:10 addition mine

For more information on Melchizedek the king/priest and how the example of him is Jesus (some believe that he is Jesus) read: Hebrews Chapter 5:6.10, Hebrews 6:20, Hebrews 7:1-21.

Now let's go on to the principle of giving, which I believe goes hand in hand with the principle of tithing.

GIVE: didōmi (did'-o-mee): A prolonged form of a primary verb (which is used as an alternate in most of the tenses); to give (used in a very wide application, properly or by implication, literally or figuratively; greatly modified by the connection): - adventure, bestow, bring forth, commit, deliver (up), give, grant, hinder, make, minister, number, offer, have power, put, receive, set, shew, smite (+ with the hand), strike (+ with the palm of the hand), suffer, take, utter, yield.

> *"Give (in) and it will be given (out) back to you..."*
> ~Luke 6:38 addition mine

This is the principle of the reciprocal saw where a blade is attached to a motor/mechanism and when touched to wood and turned on the blade will go in and out over and over and over again eventually cutting the piece of wood without ever having to move the saw blade to accomplished its purpose. That is the law of reciprocity. There is not a lot of work on the part of the giver other than giving—the motor (God) does His part as we lay out blade (by faith on the wood) and reap what we sowed.

Back in the '70s, Oral Roberts spoke of this principle under the name of "Seed Faith." He was attacked for the suggestion that you could expect God to reward your actions of sowing by allowing you to reap what you sowed. Of course God spoke about this principle back in Genesis (way before Oral Roberts).

> *"While the earth remains, Seedtime and harvest, and cold and heat, and summer and winter, And day and night shall not cease."*
> ~Genesis 8:22

This speaks of the cyclical action and reaction of nature. Seed time is the planting, and harvesting is the reaction. You planted, cultivated, and expected a harvest. As Oral Roberts use to say, "Expect a miracle."

> *"Cast thy bread upon the waters: for thou shalt find it after many days."*
> ~Ecclesiastes 11:1 (KJV)

The part about casting is our part, the waves do the rest—or the God directive waves does the rest—by bringing back to you bread on every wave. The casting is the sowing and the wave delivery system is reaping mechanism.

> *"Now I say, He (the sower) who sows sparingly (the amount sown) will also reap (return) sparingly (the ration which was sown will be returned), and he who sows bountifully (a lot( will also reap bountifully (a lot)."*
> ~II Corinthians 9:6 addition mine

NOTE: This is in written in relation to giving money and expected return.

> *"For each one (the individual giving/sowing) must do just as he has purposed in his heart (about giving a little or giving a lot), not grudgingly (with an attitude) or under compulsion (no one can force you to give anything) for God loves a cheerful (hilarious) giver."*
> ~II Corinthians 9:7 addition mine

CHEERFUL) hilaros (hil-ar-os')=From the same as G2436; propitious or merry ("hilarious"), that is, prompt or willing: - cheerful. G2436: hileōs (hil'-eh-oce)= cheerful (as attractive), that is, propitious; adverbially (by Hebraism) God be gracious!, that is, (in averting some calamity) far be it: - be it far, merciful.

This thing called giving should be:
1. Hilarious
2. Merry
3. Prompt and willing
4. Cheerful
5. Graciously
6. Merciful

One aspect of this type of giving is like joy when averting some calamity, which you will be doing as poverty is coming towards you.

*"God is able..."*
~II Corinthians 9:8

When you walk by faith and not by sight, this statement is critical God is able.

ABLE: dunatos (doo-nat-os')=From G1410; powerful or capable (literally or figuratively); neuter possible: - able, could, (that is) mighty (man), possible, power, strong. G1410: dunamai (doo'-nam-ahee)=Of uncertain affinity; to be able or possible: - be able, can (do, + -not), could, may, might, be possible, be of power.

This word able is rooted in the word for power, dynamic ability, duNAmis.

*"...to make all grace abound to you, so that always having all sufficiency in everything, you may have and abundance for every good deed."*
~II Corinthians 9:8

SUFFICENCY: autarkeia (ow-tar'-ki-ah)=From G842; self satisfaction, that is, (abstractly) contentedness, or (concretely) a competence: - contentment, sufficiency. G842: autarkēs (ow-tar'-kace)= self complacent, that is, contented: - content.

ABUNDANCE: perisseuō (per-is-syoo'-o)=From G4053; to superabound (in quantity or quality), be in excess, be superfluous; also (transitively) to cause to superabound or excel: - (make, more) abound, (have, have more) abundance, (be more) abundant, be the better, enough and to spare, exceed, excel, increase, be left, redound, remain (over and above).

G4053: perissos (per-is-sos')= in the sense of beyond), superabundant (in quantity) or superior (in quality); by implication excessive; adverb (with G1537) violently; neuter (as noun) preeminence: - exceeding abundantly above, more abundantly, advantage, exceedingly, very highly, beyond measure, more, superfluous, vehement [-ly].

When you release your money you will get money in return and be able to give again. That is why God is known as the rewarder and supplier.

> *"He scattered abroad, He gave to the poor, His righteousness endures forever."*
> ~II Corinthians 9:9, Psalm 112:9

Where do we get the seed to sow in the first place? God.

> *"Now He who supplies seed to the sower and bread for food will supply and multiply your seed for sowing and increase the harvest of your righteousness; you will be enriched in everything for all liberality, which through us is producing thanksgiving to God."*
> ~II Corinthians 9:10-11

LIBERALLY: haplotēs (hap-lot'-ace) = From G573; singleness, that is, (subjectively) sincerity (without dissimulation or self-seeking), or (objectively) generosity (copious bestowal): - bountifulness, liberal (-ity), simplicity, singleness.

Our God is not a chintzy God who trickles out supplies to us based on human ability, but based on His riches in glory in Christ Jesus. He liberally fills to the full our needs.

> *"And my God will liberally supply (fill to the full) your every need according to His riches in glory in Christ Jesus."*
> ~Philippians 4:19 (AMP)

One last example for now is found in Galatians 6:7.

> *"Do not be deceived, God is not mocked, for whatever a man sows, this he will also reap."*
> ~Galatians 6:7

Notice that the principle of sowing and reaping is not limited to money, or deeds (good or bad). "Whatever a man sows...this he will also reap."

SOWS: speirō (spi'-ro)= Probably strengthened from G4685 (through the idea of extending); to scatter, that is, sow (literally or figuratively): - sow (-er), receive seed. G4685: spaō (spah'-o)=A primary verb; to draw: - draw (out).

REAP: theridō (ther-id'-zo)=From G2330 (in the sense of the crop); to harvest: - reap. G2330: theros (ther'-os)=From a primary word therō (to heat); properly heat, that is, summer: - summer.

In your giving you will sow either to the flesh (your carnality, evil heart) or you will sow to the Spirit (in your human heart, your good, believing heart that clings to that seed with perseverance until the harvest comes.

*"But the seed (whatever you give/sow) in the good soil (heart) these are the ones who have heard the word in an honest and good heart, and hold it fast, and bear fruit with perseverance."*
Luke 8:15

"For the one who sows to his own flesh will from the flesh reap corruption, but the one who sows to the Spirit will from the Spirit reap eternal life."
~Galatians 6:8

Don't be surprised when you sow green beans and carrots don't show up. Whatever you sow, money, time, negativity, positivity will be the crop you harvest. Weeds have just as deep of roots as corn.

When they repent, turn and bring back into the storehouse what they have withheld by withholding and robbing God, the essence is that they are reversing the curse including a financial curse.

The bottom line with this tithing and giving principle is that we have seen that money is good, and love of money is bad. God gives the power to be wealthy and when God gives it, it comes without sorrow. The question is not that you have wealth but what you do with the wealth? The bottom of the bottom line is, that it is all God's in the first place and as we give, He allows us to keep the lion's share of the money with a 10/90 ratio and as you give you keep on getting so you can give again.

I have never seen someone who is living the maximized, overcoming, more than conqueror, abundant, blessed, successful, prosperous lifestyle who is not a giver or sower. This is what Andrew Carnegie wrote about in *The Gospel of Wealth*. Use your wealth and meet the needs of the poor.

Brenda and I have been married, as of this writing, 49 years. For 49 years we have practiced the principle of tithing, and we have never missed a meal or a bill and have seen increase in our finances to the point of not only being able to tithe, we were able to give as the Lord lead us. I do believe that tithing is an Old Testament principle for the Jewish people, God's chosen people. Jesus, when He spoke to the Jewish people (Jesus was a Jew by race and religion) His emphasis for them was properly the practice of tithing with the right motives.

> *"Woe to you, scribes and Pharisees, hypocrites! For you tithe mint and dill and cumin, and have neglected the weightier provisions of the Law: justice and mercy and faithfulness; but these are the things you should have done without neglecting the others."*
> ~Matthew 23:23

I believe for our purpose that we (Gentiles) are released from the tithe (10 %) to giving (100%) as the Lord lets us use the rest for our needs.

# CHAPTER FIFTEEN

## THE FORMULA FOR LIFE PRINCIPLE

In this life we live in a cursed and fallen world as a result of high treason and disobedience in the Garden by Adam and Even. That is why there is so much struggle and hardship as we attempt to live a maximized, overcoming, more than conqueror, abundant, blessed, successful, prosperous lifestyle. If it was easy then anyone would do it. In the struggle it takes vision and tenacity to remove the obstacles in our lives so that our potential can be released, and we will live in full vitality.

Many year ago I, along with my wife, Brenda, and some friends, sat under the teaching of a biochemist who taught principles for living our lives out victoriously maximizing our full potential. The biochemist said, "Professor Arnold Ehret wrote in 1922, *Vitality equals power, minus obstruction.*"

It is one of those things that has stuck with me until this day as I write this chapter.

$V = P - O$

The breakdown of this formula is:

V= Vitality: (1) exuberant physical strength or mental vigor (2) capacity for survival or for the continuation of a meaningful or purposeful existence (3) power to live or grow (4) vital force or principle

P= Potential: (1) possible, as opposed to actual (2) capable of being or becoming (3) possibility; potentiality (4) a latent excellence or ability that may or may not be developed

O= Obstructions: a latent excellence or ability that may or may not be developed (2) an act or instance of obstructing (3) an act or instance of obstructing.

To obstruct mean: (1) to block or close up with an obstacle; make difficult to pass (2) to interrupt, hinder, or oppose the passage, progress, course, etc., of (3) to block from sight; to be in the way of (a view, passage, etc.)

Everyone faces the obstructions in life and everyone has a choice to just accept the obstructions of move the obstructions.

This thing called vitality was present at the original creation. God purposed us in His mind and manifested His thought with the creation of man; male and female. There was freedom in this unobstructed potential as they were created with vitality. These created beings had exuberant vigor, a capacity for survival, the ability to continue with a meaningful and purposeful existence, and power to live with the principle of vital force.

This vital couple were place in the Garden of Eden and given instructions on how to live an obstruction free existence. All they had to do was obey their Creator.

> *"The Lord God, commanded the man, saying from any tree of the garden you may earth freely, but from the tree of the knowledge of good and evil you shall not eat, for in that day (that you eat) from it you shall surely die."*
>
> ~Genesis 2:16-17 addition mine

The obstacle came in the form of a serpent (over who they had authority) and their choice to walk in disobedience; walk in high treason. (Genesis 3:1-7) When the serpent creeped into the garden, he planted doubt in the mind of the woman. (Genesis 2:3)

The problem arose for them and the rest of mankind and womankind when she did not exercise her God-given authority to deal the obstacle (doubt, the lust of the eyes, flesh and pride) and the obstacle-bearer (the serpent). Of course the man (the head covering for the wife) was there, had passed on the commands, and was close enough to take a bite of the fruit when the woman offered it to him. They both had the authority over the obstacles, so they could remain in full vitality. (Romans 3:6-11)

The cause and effect rippled down in a tsunami wave (an unusually large sea wave produced by a seaquake or undersea volcanic eruption) that reached the whole world (humans) from then until now.

> *"Therefore, just as through one man (Adam) sin entered into the world, and death (physical and spiritual cause and effect) through sin (the ultimate obstacle keeping us from full vitality), so death (cause and effect) spread to all men because all sinned."*
> ~Romans 5:12 addition mine

When God showed up on the scene for their regularly scheduled time of fellowship in the garden, he quizzed Adam about what they had done (knowing all along what was done). (Genesis 3:8-10)

When Adam 'fessed up, God continue the line of questioning and that is when the name game, the passing of the buck started. (Genesis 3:12-13)

> *"The man said, "the woman whom You gave to be with me she gave me from the tree, and I ate."*
> ~Genesis 3:12

NOTE: This is known as a two-for blame as Adam blamed (1) the woman (2) God who gave him the woman.

God then turns His attention on the woman who after Adam tagged her (you're it), blamed the serpent.

> *"...the serpent deceived me and I ate."*
> ~Genesis 3:13

To paraphrase the Sonny and Cher song, "The Beat Goes On," *thatr beat just keeps goings on...throughout history.*

If you are going to live a maximized, overcoming, more than conqueror, victorious, abundant, successful, and prosperous lifestyle, you will have to cease and desist obstructing the way to your full potential and depleted vitality by disobeying God with sin and blaming the other guy for your failure.

## CHAPTER SIXTEEN

## THE LIVING WATER PRINCIPLE

We have talked about how we are made up of three parts as one unit. Each part on its own is complete, but when all three are working together as one unit there is a synergistic quality to man, woman, humans. As we saw in the previous chapter, we were created to have vitality, but our full potential cannot be reached on our own means.

> *"Now may the God (Creator) of peace (wholeness, rest, brought to one again) Himself sanctify (set you apart for a purpose) you entirely (wholly) and may your spirit, soul and body be preserved complete, without blame at the coming of our Lord Jesus Christ."*
> ~I Thessalonians 5:23 addition mine

SPIRIT: pneuma (pnyoo'-mah)=From G4154; a current of air, that is, breath (blast) or a breeze; by analogy or figuratively a spirit, that is, (human) the rational soul, (by implication) vital principle, mental disposition, etc., or (superhuman) an angel, daemon, or (divine) God, Christ's spirit, the Holy spirit: - ghost, life, spirit (-ual, -ually), mind. G415: pneō (pneh'-o)=A primary word; to breathe hard, that is, breeze: - blow.

SPIRIT: psuchō (psoo'-kho)=A primary verb; to breathe (voluntarily but gently; thus differing on the one hand from G4154, which denotes properly a forcible respiration; and on the other from the base of G109, which refers properly to an inanimate breeze), that is, (by implication of reduction of temperature by evaporation) to chill (figuratively): - wax cold.

SPIRIT: neshâmâh (nesh-aw-maw')=From H5395; a puff, that is, wind, angry or vital breath, divine inspiration, intellect or (concretely) an animal: - blast, (that) breath (-eth), inspiration, soul, spirit. H5395: nâsham (naw-sham')=A primitive root; properly to blow away, that is, destroy: - destroy.

The initial creation of man and the subsequent creation of woman all started out with God forming man out of dust (along with mist from the earth) from the ground. (Genesis 3:7) God then took this shape of clay and breathed his breath into the nostrils, and the cause and effect was man became a living being. (Genesis 3:7)

BREATHED: nâphach (naw-fakh')=A primitive root; to puff, in various applications (literally, to inflate, blow hard, scatter, kindle, expire; figuratively, to disesteem): - blow, breath, give up, cause to lose [life], seething, snuff.

BREATH: neshâmâh (nesh-aw-maw')= a puff, that is, wind, angry or vital breath, divine inspiration, intellect or (concretely) an animal: - blast, (that) breath (-eth), inspiration, soul, spirit.

LIFE: chay (khah'ee)= alive; hence raw (flesh); fresh (plant, water, year), strong; also (as noun, especially in the feminine singular and masculine plural) life (or living thing), whether literally or figuratively: - + age, alive, appetite, (wild) beast, company, congregation, life (-time), live (-ly), living (creature, thing), maintenance, + merry, multitude, + (be) old, quick, raw, running, springing, troop.

LIVING: chay (khah'ee)=alive; hence raw (flesh); fresh (plant, water, year), strong; also (as noun, especially in the feminine singular and masculine plural) life (or living thing), whether literally or figuratively: - + age, alive, appetite, (wild) beast, company, congregation, life (-time), live (-ly), living (creature, thing), maintenance, + merry, multitude, + (be) old, quick, raw, running, springing, troop.

SOUL/BEING: nephesh (neh'-fesh)= properly a breathing creature, that is, animal or (abstractly) vitality; used very widely in a literal, accommodated or figurative sense (bodily or mental): - any, appetite, beast, body, breath, creature, X dead (-ly), desire, X [dis-] contented, X fish, ghost, + greedy, he, heart (-y), (hath, X jeopardy of) life (X in jeopardy), lust, man, me, mind, mortality, one, own, person, pleasure, (her-, him-, my-, thy-) self, them (your) -selves, + slay, soul, + tablet, they, thing, (X she) will, X would have it.

I believe that in Genesis 3:7 we see the introduction of a physical body, soul and the spirit. We see the cause and effect of the breath of God, The Holy Spirit (the big S) creating the human spirit (little s).

*"The spirit of man is the lamp of the LORD, Searching all the innermost parts of his being."*
~Pro-Verb 20:27

NOTE: In some translations this lamp is called "the candle of the Lord." Back in the original days there were no candles, only oil lamps.

The human spirit (little) is the man component of the creation of God, spirit, soul, and body. In the original state of creation the human was created at full capacity and vitality (See chapter Nine on The Formula For Life Principle).

This lamp, this human spirit is deep within in the core of the body. In the New Testament our body, our physical being is known as the temple/sanctuary/inner room of the Holy Spirit. (I Corinthians 3:16, I Corinthians 6:19-20)

When man/woman/Adam/Eve sinned with disobedience and high treason, we were cursed with death (spiritually and physically) and in essence we were sold into slavery. Jesus came to buy us back out of slavery with the ransom of His death and the victory of His resurrection.

When sin, the obstacle, entered in, it blocked the potential for a return to maximum vitality. Something had to happen as cataclysmic as the fall to reverse the curse.

That thing that happened was Jesus dying on the cross in our place, being buried and then rising from the dead on the third day. (I Corinthians 15:1-5)

Prior to Jesus' departure, He spoke of what would happen when He went back to the Father in heaven. What happened would prime the pump of the spirit (little s) with an outflow of The Holy Spirit (the big S).

> *"I will ask the Father, and He will give you another Helper, that He may be with your forever, that is the Spirit of truth whom the world cannot receive, because it does not see Him or know Him, but you know Him because He abides with you and will be in you."*
> ~John 14:16-17

Jesus had gone to a great feast that was traditional in Jewish customs. It was known as the Feast of Booths.

"The Feast of Tabernacles, also sometimes called the Feast of Booths in some translations, is one of the biblical holidays described in Leviticus 23. Jewish people do not typically refer to it as "the Feast of Tabernacles" (or "Booths"), but more commonly refer to it by its Hebrew name: Sukkot." FDrom *First Fruits of Zion*, https://ffoz.org/

"…the Jews had a ceremony of carrying water from the Pool of Siloam and pouring it into a silver basin by the altar of burnt offering each day for the first seven days of the Feast of Booths. On the eight day this was not done, making Christs' offer of the water of eternal life from Himself even more startling." Ryrie Study Bible note on John 7:37-30

Picture the procession, the pomp and circumstance of the water being paraded into the altar and poured out upon the altar for seven days. On the eight day, when no water was being poured, Jesus stood up and cried out loud (calling attention to himself,

> *"If anyone (whosoever) is thirsty, let him come to Me and drink."*
> ~John 7:37

Not only would Jesus satisfy their thirst (spiritual and physical) there would be a cause and effect of drinking His water. The key is to believe (trust in, cling to, rely on, adhere to) in Jesus. The cause and effect would be the priming of the pump (the innermost being, the belly) will flow (not trickle out) rivers (stream) of living waters (alive, active).

> *"Ho! (Hey, listen up) Everyone who thirsts, come to the waters; and you who have no money come, buy and eat. Come, buy wine and mike without money and without cost."*
>
> ~Isaiah 55:2 addition mine

Isaiah is speaking of an everlasting covenant being made which in reality was our everlasting covenant with the water giver, Jesus. (Isaiah 55:3, John 7:37-38)

> *"Then he brought me back to the door of the house; and behold, water was flowing from under the threshold of the house toward the east, for the house faced east. And the water was flowing down from under, from the right side of the house, from south of the altar. He brought me out by way of the north gate and led me around on the outside to the outer gate by way of the gate that faces east. And behold, water was trickling from the south side. When the man went out toward the east with a line in his hand, he measured a thousand cubits, and he led me through the water, water reaching the ankles. Again he measured a thousand and led me through the water, water reaching the knees. Again he measured a thousand and led me through the water, water reaching the loins. Again he measured a thousand; and it was a river that I could not ford, for the water had risen, enough water to swim in, a river that could not be forded."*
>
> ~Ezekiel 47: 1-7

Water flowed from the altar of the temple starting out a trickle and then went ankle, to knee to swimming levels as a deep river. The cause and effect of the river of water flowing from the temple will cause tree growth and even sweeten the waters of the Dead see to the point that fish will live in it. (Ezekiel 47:1-12) This speaks to me of rivers of living water flowing out of the innermost being.

Jesus defined what these rivers (plural) of living waters were—the Holy Spirit.

> *"But this He spoke of the Spirit, whom those who believed in Him were to receive; for the Spirit was not yet given, because Jesus was not yet glorified."*
>
> ~John 7:39

The one who has the Holy Spirit and has the Holy Spirit flow out of him will be the one who will be living the maximized, overcoming, more than conqueror, victorious, abundant, successful and prosperous lifestyle. The person who can say that Jesus is Lord by the Holy Spirit (I Corinthians 12:3) is the same person who has The Spirit of God dwelling in the lamp of the Lord. It is this lamp (the little s, spirit) that the gifts of the Spirit flow (Corinthians 12:8-11) and where the fruit of the Spirit grows (Galatians 5:22-23)

This Holy Spirit (Big S) who dwells in the human spirit (little s) is the same Holy Spirit who:
1. helps our weaknesses
2. knows how to pray when we don't
3. intercedes for us with a groaning that is too deep for words
4. searches the hearts
5. knows what the mind of the Spirit is
6. intercedes for us (the saints) according to the will of God. (Romans 8:26-27)

In my mind that is a major advantage for success in all that we put our hand to.

There are things that mere mortal man cannot fathom.

> *"…things which eye has not seen and ear has not heard and which have not entered the heart of man, all that God has prepared for those who love Him."*
>
> ~I Corinthians 2:9

So how are these things revealed to us?

> *"For to us God revealed them through the Spirit (Big S); for even the Spirit searches all things, even the depths of God (Romans 8:26-27) For who among men knows the thoughts of a man except the spirit (little s) of the man? Even so, the thoughts of God no one knows except the Spirit (Big S) of God. Now we have received not the spirit of the world, but the Spirit (Big S) who is from God, so that we may know the things freely given to us by God, which things we also speak not in words taught by human wisdom, but in those taught by the Spirit, combining spiritual thoughts with spiritual words."*
> ~I Corinthians 2:10-13 addition mine

Now that is what I call an advantage in the natural world and in the spiritual world. When a man has the Holy Spirit dwelling inside him, with the gifts of the spirit like the word of knowledge, the word of wisdom, and discerning of spirits, people can be touched.

If you fell in a river, came out of the river, and hugged someone, they will get wet. When you are flowing in the Spirit with the rivers of living water flowing out of you, whoever comes into contact with you will feel the effects of the Spirit.

If you live like this daily, you are living the maximized, overcoming, more than conqueror, victorious, abundant, successful, prosperous lifestyle.

## THE BLESSING PRICIPLE

BLESSED (beyond the curse, yes Lord). In a cursed and dying world the tendency is that it is a sin to be blessed.

BLESSED: makarios (mak-ar'-ee-os)=A prolonged form of the poetical makar (meaning the same); supremely blest; by extension fortunate, well off: - blessed, happy (X -ier).

In the Beatitudes (be the attitudes that we need to be having), The

Amplified Bible expands the thought of being blessed. (Matthew 5:1-9) Jesus speaks of being blessed nine times.
1. Happy, to be envied, spiritually prosperous with life-joy satisfaction in God's favor and satisfaction, *regardless* of their outward conditions. (Matthew 5:3)
2. Enviably happy with a happiness produced by the experience of God's favor and especially conditioned by the revelation of His matchless grace. (Matthew 5:2)
3. Happy, blithesome, joyous, spiritually prosperous with life joy and satisfaction in God's favor and salvation. (Matthew 5:5)
4. Fortunate and happy and spiritually prosperous in that state in which the born-again child of God enjoys His favor and salvation, *regardless* of their outward condition. (Matthew 5:6)
5. Happy to be envied and spiritually prosperous with life-joy and satisfaction in God's favor and salvation, *regardless* of their outward conditions.
6. Happy, enviably fortunate and spiritually prosperous possessing the happiness produced by the experience of God's favor and especially conditioned by the revelation of His grace, regardless of their outward condition. (Matthew 5:8)
7. Enjoying enviable happiness, spiritually prosperous with life-joy and satisfaction in God's favor and salvation, *regardless* of their outward condition. (Matthew 5:9)
8. Happy and enviably fortunate and spiritually prosperous in the state in which the born against child of God enjoys and finds satisfaction in God's favor and salvation, *regardless* of his outward conditions. (Matthew 5:10)
9. Happy, to be envied and spiritually prosperous with life-joy and satisfaction in God's favor and salvation, *regardless* of you outward conditions. (Matthew 5:11)

The ones who find the *Blessing Regardless Of Their Outward Condition*
1. The poor in spirit (theirs is the kingdom of heaven)
2. Those who mourn (they shall be comforted)
3. The meek, mild, patient, long-suffering (they shall inherit the earth)

4. Those who hunger and thirst for righteousness (they shall filled)
5. The merciful (they shall obtain mercy)
6. The pure in heart (they shall see God)
7. Peace makers (they shall be called the sons of God)
8. Those who are persecuted for righteousness sake (for theirs is the kingdom of heaven)
9. When people revile and persecute you and say all kinds of evil against you falsely *on my account* (their reward is in heaven).

No doubt the outward condition is bad but *Regardless Of Their Outward Condition*, the expectation is *blessings*, not just in the pie in the sky but in the nitty gritty now. The access is not by sight but by faith *Regardless Of The Outward Condition* (II Corinthians 5:7)

Blessing is not just financial (I acknowledge I am blessed financially), but it is physical, emotional, and spiritual. When I see someone that is blessed, they are enviable, like Jesus said we would be. I don't apologize for *not* living a cursed life here on earth.

# CHAPTER SEVENTEEN

## THE LOVE PRINCIPLE

*"I love it when a plan comes together."*
~Hannibal Smith of the A-Team

Who would have thought that when chapter thirteen rolled around that I would be talking about The Love Principle found in I Corinthians 13, also known as *The Love Chapter*?

Larry Norman, the father of Christian Rock and Roll states, "without love you ain't nothing."

If anyone tries to live a maximized, overcoming, more than conqueror, victorious, abundant, blessed, successful, prosperous lifestyle and tries to bypass The Love Principle, they will automatically default to The Lust Principle.

Epithumia (ep-ee-thoo-mee'-ah)= From G1937; a longing (especially for what is forbidden): - concupiscence, desire, lust (after). G1937: epithumeō (ep-ee-thoo-meh'-o)= to set the heart upon, that is, long for (rightfully or otherwise): - covet, desire, would fain, lust (after).

This Lust Principle is nothing new. It was in the Garden of Eden with Adam and Eve (Genesis 3:1-7) and in the wilderness with Jesus. (Matthew 4:1-11, Luke 4:1-14) If you think that the d-evil won't tempt you with The Lust Principle like he did with God's crown of creation (man/woman) and Jesus Himself, you are mistaken.

*"For all that is in the world, the lust of the flesh and the lust of*

*the eyes and the boastful pride of life, is not from the Father, but is from the world."*

~I John 2:16

*"But now faith, hope, love abide these three; but the greatest of these is love."*

~I Corinthians 13:13

FAITH: pistis (pis'-tis) = From G3982; persuasion, that is, credence; moral conviction (of religious truth, or the truthfulness of God or a religious teacher), especially reliance upon Christ for salvation; abstractly constancy in such profession; by extension the system of religious (Gospel) truth itself: - assurance, belief, believe, faith, fidelity. G3982: pistis (pis'-tis) =From G3982; persuasion, that is, credence; moral conviction (of religious truth, or the truthfulness of God or a religious teacher), especially reliance upon Christ for salvation; abstractly constancy in such profession; by extension the system of religious (Gospel) truth itself: - assurance, belief, believe, faith, fidelity.

HOPE : elpis (el-pece') =From elpō which is a primary word (to anticipate, usually with pleasure); expectation (abstract or concrete) or confidence: - faith, hope.

LOVE: agapē (ag-ah'-pay)=From G25; love, that is, affection or benevolence G25: agapaō (ag-ap-ah'-o)=to love (in a social or moral sense): - (be-) love (-ed).

What is interesting to me is the love/faith relationship. Yes, according to I Corinthians 13:13 the greatest of the three (faith, hope, love) is love, however if you think about it, you can't truly love the unlovable without faith and faith is how love works.

*"For in Jesus Christ neither circumcision availeth anything, nor uncircumcision; but faith which worketh by love."*

~Galatians 5:6 (KJV)

Love is the great motivator and faith is the great believer while hope gives that confident expectation that faith hooks into as it loves.

Of course the greatest example of love was the love that God had for the world as He gave his Son and the love that the Son had for the Father as He laid it all on the cross for us whom He (Jesus) loves.

*"He (Jesus) who has My commandments and keeps them, he it is who loves me and he who loves Me (Jesus) will be loved by My (Jesus) Father (God) and I (Jesus) will love him and will disclose, reveal and manifest Myself (Jesus) to him."*
~John 14:21 addition mine

While John 3:16 is the center point of the Bible (not physically but spiritually) God's love is mentioned much earlier than Jesus.

In the Bible there are at least 281 verses on love with love mentioned 311 times (E-Sword search for the word love)

One of my favorite verses on His love towards us is found in Lamentations 3:22.

*"The steadfast love of the Lord never ceases, for His compassions never fail. They are new every morning; great is your faithfulness."*
~Lamentations 3:22

The Jews, God's chosen people, had a history of turning to idols for help instead of turning to God. The Babylonian armies had overrun them and captured them. Babylon's grip tightened on these *chosen people*, and they were starving, but they still continue to turn to idols for their needs. Now, before you shake your head at the actions of the children of Israel, realize how we do the same thing in our daily lives. The great deportation had taken place, and as Jeremiah the prophet has seen all of these things happen, he wrote what has come to be known as Lamentations. The word lamentation mean to cry aloud. According to the introduction notes to Lamentations the book attributed to Jeremiah, "consist of five melancholy poems of mourning over the utter destruction of Jerusalem and the temple by the Babylonians."

In the mist of the laments is a breath of hope, confident expectation.

> *"Therefore, I have hope in Him."*
> ~Lamentations 3:24

I believe that The Love Principle found in this book is key to hope and deliverance even in this day and age.

The feeling from the prophet is that his soul had been rejected from peace. He had forgotten happiness, his strength had perished and so had his hope. (Lamentations 3:17-18) His lack of hope cries out for the Lord to remember his affliction, his wandering and the wormwood and the bitterness that his soul remembers and is bowed down within him.

> *This I recall to my mind, therefore I have hope. The steadfast love (loving kindnesses) of the Lord never cease (comes to an end), for His compassion (mercies) never fail. They are new every morning; great is your faithfulness.*
> ~Lamentations 3: 17-23

> *"…therefore (because of the remembrance of his soul, I have hope."*
> ~Lamentations 3:24

In the Greek language there are four main words for the word love. C.S. Lewis famed Christian apologist, former atheist, philosopher, professor and author had a radio address and book entitled *The Four Loves*. "The book was based on a set of radio talks from 1958 which had been criticized in the U.S. at the time for their frankness about sex." (Wikipedia)

> *"I love hotdogs, my pet and my wife, not necessarily in that order."*
> ~Rodney Boyd

Each word for love is true, but the meanings are vastly different. As stated above in the Greek language there are four words for the word love.

1. Storge': This is a word of empathy or a familial love. Storge' is the love of a mother for a child. I remember it by thinking of a stork delivering a baby.
2. Philia: This is a friend/brotherly love. Philia is where we get the word where we get the name Philadelphia (city of brotherly love)
3. Eros: This is an erotic or sensual love. Eros, erotic and sensual does not mean only sexual but a love that excites the senses, like I love hot dogs. Eros out of control is lust or called Eros defiled.
4. Agape': This is an unconditional God like love. Agape' is the God kind of love that we are to have towards others and our brothers and sisters in love. When or Agape' love becomes looesy-goosey, it becomes what is known as sloppy Agape'.

Each of these love in themselves is not bad but actually good. But when they are not under control of Agape' the love turns into lust.

*"For God so greatly loved (Agape') and dearly prized the world that he (even) gave up His only begotten (unique, first born among many sons and daughters) Son, so that whoever believes in (trusts in clings to relies on) Him shall not perish but have eternal (everlasting) life."*
~John 3:16 (AMP) addition mine

In our chapter about The Faith Principle we saw that our faith towards God is an elementary principle. Once we have experienced our love from God, then we direct our faith towards others.

*"But God shows and clearly proves His [own] love for (towards) us by the fact that while we were yet (still) sinners, Christ (Jesus, the Messiah, the Anointed One) died for us."*
~Romans 5:8 (AMP) addition mine

*Just like our faith without corresponding works is of none affect (dead), so is our love with expression towards those who don't deserve it is of none effect.*
~James 2:17 paraphrased addition mine

Jesus, when was quizzed on what is the most important law, responded by referring to love.

> *"Jesus answered, the first and principal commandment is hear O Israel, the Lord our God is one Lord; and you shall love the Lord your God out of and with your whole heart and out of and with all your soul (your life) and out of and with all your mind (your faculty of thought and your moral understanding) and out of and with all your strength. This is the first and principle commandment. The second is like it and is this, you shall love your neighbor as yourself. There is no other commandment greater than these."*
> ~Mark 12:29-31 (AMP) addition mine

If you are going to live a maximized, overcoming, more than conqueror, victorious, abundant, successful, prosperous lifestyle, you are going to have to walk in the Principle of Love.

## CHAPTER EIGHTEEN

## THE VICTORY PRINCIPLE

By now I hope that you are getting the idea that failure is not something that you should aspire to unless you are failing in your own attempts to BE victorious as you die to your own plans and live unto His plans for you.

The key to true victory, the real Victory Principle is found in the resurrected life.

> "Behold, I tell you a mystery (now revealed); we will not all sleep, but will be changed, in a moment, in the twinkling of an eye, at the last trumpet; for the trumpet will sound and the dead will be raised imperishable and we will be changed. For this perishable must put on the imperishable, and this mortal must put on immortality. But when this perishable will have put on the imperishable and this mortal will have put on immortality, then will come about the saying that is written, 'death is swallowed up in victory. O death where is your victory? O death, where is your sting? The sting of death is sin and the power of sin is the law; but thanks be to God, who gives us the victory through our Lord Jesus Christ."
> ~I Corinthians 15:51-57

The true victory here on this earth in this present moment will be fully realized in the future, but the present still affects our now. True victory is supernatural that affects our natural until He returns to take us away to our real home.

As we walk by faith (here presently) we will see the great exchange from mortality to immortality, from this present (earthly tent) to the future (heavenly building of God) we can be of good courage.

> "For indeed, while we are in this tent (flesh body), we groan being burdened, because we do not want to be unclothed but to be clothed, so that what is mortal will be swallowed up by life. Now He who prepared us for this very purpose (to be immortal) is god, who gave us the Spirit (Holy) as a pledge. Therefore, being always of good courage, and knowing that while we are at home in the body and to be at home with the Lord. Therefore we also have as our ambition, whether at home or absent, to be pleasing to Him."
> ~II Corinthians 5:4-9 addition mine

It is only when we realize that we can fit into the victorious plans that God has for us.

> "For I know the plans that I have for you,' declares the LORD, 'plans for welfare and not for calamity to give you a future and a hope."
> ~Jeremiah 29:11

So while we are here on planet Earth we are to conduct ourselves by faith as we regulate our lives and conduct ourselves. (II Corinthians 5:7) Because of our victorious mindset we are to be and act a certain way.

Therefore, because of the mortality/immortality and the perishable/imperishable mindset and because the death sting of sin and the power of sin is nullified, our God gives us the victory through Christ Jesus (I Corinthians 15:51-57).

> "Therefore, my beloved brethren, be steadfast, immovable, always abounding in the work of the Lord, knowing that your toil is not in vain in the Lord."
> ~I Corinthians 15:58

In other words we can live in victory, in Jesus.

> "For I know the thoughts and plans that I have for you, says the

*Lord, thoughts and plans for welfare and peace and not for evil, to give you hope in our final outcome."*
~Jeremiah 29:11 (AMP)

PLANS/THOUGHTS: (machăshâbâh machăshebeth (makh-ash-aw-baw', makh-ash-eh'-beth)=From H2803; a contrivance, that is, (concretely) a texture, machine, or (abstractly) intention, plan (whether bad, a plot; or good, advice): - cunning (work), curious work, device (-sed), imagination, invented, means, purpose, thought. H2803: châshab (khaw-shab')=A primitive root; properly to plait or interpenetrate, that is, (literally) to weave or (generally) to fabricate; figuratively to plot or contrive (usually in a malicious sense); hence (from the mental effort) to think, regard, value, compute: - (make) account (of), conceive, consider, count, cunning (man, work, workman), devise, esteem, find out, forecast, hold, imagine, impute, invent, be like, mean, purpose, reckon (-ing be made), regard, think.

PEACE: shâlôm (shaw-lome', shaw-lome')=From H7999; safe, that is, (figuratively) well, happy, friendly; also (abstractly) welfare, that is, health, prosperity, peace: - X do, familiar, X fare, favour, + friend, X greet, (good) health, (X perfect, such as be at) peace (-able, -ably), prosper (-ity, -ous), rest, safe (-ly), salute, welfare, (X all is, be) well, X wholly. H799: shâlam (shaw-lam')=A primitive root; to be safe (in mind, body or estate); figuratively to be (causatively make) completed; by implication to be friendly; by extension to reciprocate (in various applications): - make amends, (make an) end, finish, full, give again, make good, (re-) pay (again), (make) (to) (be at) peace (-able), that is perfect, perform, (make) prosper (-ous), recompense, render, requite, make restitution, restore, reward, X surely.

EVIL: (rah, raw-aw') =bad or (as noun) evil (naturally or morally). This includes the second (feminine) form; as adjective or noun: - adversity, affliction, bad, calamity, + displease (-ure), distress, evil ([-favouredness], man, thing), + exceedingly, X great, grief (-vous), harm, heavy, hurt (-ful), ill (favoured), + mark, mischief, (-vous), misery, naught (-ty), noisome, + not please, sad (-ly), sore, sorrow, trouble, vex, wicked (-ly, -ness, one), worse (-st) wretchedness, wrong. [Including feminine ra'ah; as adjective or noun.]

Jeremiah 29:11 was written while Israel was in exile into Babylon because they opened the door by being disobedient to the Lord. But God's plans and thoughts were not their plans and thoughts.

> *"For My thoughts are not your thoughts, or are your ways My ways," declares the LORD. "For as the heavens are higher than the earth, or are My ways higher than your ways And My thoughts than your thoughts."*
> ~Isaiah 55:9-10

We tend to take our thoughts, make our plans, and then try to get God to go along with our thoughts and plans. When our plans crash and burn we blame it on God or the d-evil or some other person when all along it was us stepping out ahead of God.

> *"Things which eye has not seen, and ear has not heard, and which have not entered the heart of man, all that God has prepared for those who love Him."*
> ~I Corinthians 2:9, Isaiah 64:5, Isaiah 65:7

When we try to make plans based on the unseen and the unheard with no heart of those things about the preparation (God's plans), why be surprised at failure.

To live a maximized, overcoming, more than conqueror, victorious, blessed, abundant, prosperous and successful lifestyle, you need a plan that aligns with God's plan. You need a revelation from God and not a revelation from you humanism.

> *"For to us God revealed them (pulled aside the curtain) through the Spirit (Holy Spirit, big S) for the spirit (human spirit, little s) searches all things, even the depths of God."*
> ~I Corinthians 2:10 addition mine

If you want to know the depths of God and His revelations you have to be linked into the Holy Spirit who knows the depths of God's plans for you.

NOTE: For more information about the Holy Spirit (Big S) and the human spirit (little s) see Chapter 12 on The Living Water Principle.

While some of the things are redundant regarding the Holy Spirit (Big S) and your human spirit (little s) it will not hurt to say the same things to you so that you may be established and solidified in your faith.

> *"Finally, my brethren, rejoice in the Lord. To write the same things again is no trouble to me, and it is a safeguard for you."*
> ~Philippians 3:1

> *"My children, with whom I am again in labor until Christ is formed in you—"*
> ~Galatians 4:19

You have God thoughts and man thoughts. When man thoughts line up with God thoughts, there is victory.

> *"For who among men knows the thoughts of a man except the spirit (little s) of the man which is in him (inside him, in his belly, in his core, in his heart, in his innermost being)? Even so (just like that) the thoughts of God (Things which eye has not seen, and ear has not heard, and which have not entered the heart of man, all that God has prepared for those who love Him) no one knows except the Spirit of God (Big S who dwells within you)."*
> ~I Corinthians 2:11 addition mine

If we are going to line up with God's thoughts so that we can have victory instead of failure we are going to have to speak God thoughts in our life.

NOTE: For more information about speaking God's thoughts and words, see Chapter Two, The Faith Principle

> *"Now we have received not the spirit of the world, but the Spirit who is from God, so that we may know (that we know, that we know, that we know) the things freely given to us by God, which things we also speak, not in words taught by human wisdom, but in those taught by the Spirit (the Teacher, John 14:26) by the Spirit, combining spiritual though with spiritual words:*
> ~I Corinthians 2:12-13 addition mine

To be someone who lives the maximized, overcoming, more than conqueror, victorious, blessed, abundant successful, prosperous life style, you are going to have to change your way of thinking, change your way of speaking which will in turn change the way you do things. Since you are a spiritual being you are going to have to live by spiritual thoughts and principle and speak spiritual thoughts in a natural world.

> *"BuT a natural man (not a born again man/woman) does not accept the things of the Spirit of God, for they are foolishness to him; and he cannot understand them, because they are spiritually appraised, But he who is spiritual appraises all things, yet he himself is appraised by no one. But who has known the mind of the Lord, that he will instruct Him? But we have the mind of Christ."*
> ~I Corinthians 2:14-16 addition mine

So once again we reinforce the fact that we can live in the maximized, overcoming, more than conqueror, victorious, abundant, blessed, successful, prosperous lifestyle.

# CHAPTER NINETEEN

## THE SUFFERING PRINCIPLE

In many people's quest for the maximized, overcoming, more than conqueror, victorious, blessed, abundant, successful, prosperous lifestyle, we are in danger of forgetting that suffering is part of the process.

"The Gospel of Wealth, is an article written by Andrew Carnegie in June of 1889 that describes the responsibility of philanthropy by the new upper class of self-made rich. Carnegie proposed that the best way of dealing with the new phenomenon of wealth inequality was for the wealthy to utilize their surplus means in a responsible and thoughtful manner." (Wikipedia on The Gospel of Wealth)

Of course, many people assume that if they would give to the poor or do other acts of good that they would be insured a place in heaven. Their works and good deeds become merit badges or their get out of hell free pass. Jesus was very clear on how to get into the presence of the Father and it was not by good works/deeds.

*"Jesus told him, "I am the way, the truth, and the life. No one comes to the Father except through me.""*

~John 14:6

Jesus did not say that, "I am a way, a truth and a life. Anyone can come to the Father through their good works and deeds and how the treat the poor and suffering." (John 14:16 twisted and perverted).

Paul underscored this thing called works/deeds as a means for salvation.

*"He (Jesus with the Death, Burial, Resurrection) saved us (from destruction, hell) not on the basis of deeds (good works, giving to the poor, helping the ones suffering) which we have done in the flesh (our own efforts) but (in contrast) according to (on the basis of) the washing of regeneration and the renewing by the Holy Spirit.( a God thing and not a man thing) "*
~Titus 3:5 addition mine

Paul also gives insight into what saves us and what does not and the place of works. There are works that are prepared for us to do but not for salvation.

*"For by grace you have been save through faith; and that not of yourselves, it is the gift of God, not as a result of works, so that no one may boast. For we are His workman ship, created in Christ Jesus for good works, which God prepared beforehand so that we would walk in them."*
~Ephesians 2:8-10

GRACE: Charis (khar'-ece) =From G5463; graciousness (as gratifying), of manner or act (abstract or concrete; literal, figurative or spiritual; especially the divine influence upon the heart, and its reflection in the life; including gratitude): - acceptable, benefit, favour, gift, grace (-ious), joy liberality, pleasure, thank (-s, -worthy). G5463: hairō (khah'ee-ro) =A primary verb; to be full of "cheer", that is, calmly happy or well off; impersonal especially as a salutation (on meeting or parting), be well: - farewell, be glad, God speed, greeting, hail, joy (-fully), rejoice.

My favorite part about this definition of grace is, "…the divine influence upon the heart and its reflection in the life…" This thing called grace is an inside-out job. The inside touch from God affects what we do outside in our flesh, the works and deeds that we do, like giving to the poor. When we are touched by God the reflection is visible in our lives. When He blesses us with the maximized, overcoming, more than conqueror, victorious, blessed, abundant, successful and prosperous lifestyle by grace on our inside, people will see the reflection how we live our lives, out loud.

In the Amplified Bible when Jesus is teaching on the Beatitudes (they be the attitude that we need to be having) (Matthew 5:12), being blessed is defined as:

1. Blessed
2. Happy
3. To be envied
4. Spiritually prosperous with lie-joy and satisfaction in God's favor and salvation, regardless of their outward conditions
5. Enviable happy with a happiness that is produced by the experience of God's favor especially conditioned by the revelation of His matchless grace
6. Blithesome (lighthearted; merry; cheerful)
7. Joyous
8. Fortunate
9. Enjoying His favor and salvation
10. Completely satisfied
11. Enviably prosperous
12. Supremely joyful.

In my travels around the world, I have found that people can be blessed and joyful living in a small shack or a hut with no walls, meeting under a tree or worshiping in the jungle without the entrapments of wealth (in the sense of our skewed view of wealth) that believers in the death, burial, and resurrection of Jesus, true believers who (trust in, cling to, rely on, adhere to) God and His Word.

One of the fallacies of Christians who are trying to convince others to become Christians is that we paint salvation as an end to the suffering in their lives. This false impression will implode when they are hit with even more suffering than they had before they became Christians. There can be blessings within the sufferings of this life.

SUFFERING: pathēma (path'-ay-mah) =From a presumed derivative of G3806; something undergone, that is, hardship or pain; subjectively an emotion or influence: - affection, affliction, motion, suffering. G3806: pathos (path'-os) =From the alternate of G3958;

properly suffering ("pathos"), that is, (subjectively) a passion (especially concupiscence): - (inordinate) affection, lust. Apparently a primary verb (the third form used only in certain tenses for it); to experience a SUFFER: paschō pathō penthō (pas'-kho, path'-o, pen'-tho) =sensation or impression (usually painful): - feel, passion, suffer, vex

Many believers, believe that to be "holy," "spiritual," or "righteous" that they must suffer. Along with this mindset is that they must be under the thumb of poverty to truly be "holy," "spiritual," or "righteous."

> *"More than that, I count (command with official authority, to deem, consider: - account, (be) chief, count, esteem, governor, judge, have the rule over, suppose, think) all things to be loss in view of the surpassing value of knowing Christ Jesus my Lord, for whom I have suffered (to injure, to experience detriment, be cast away, receive damage, lose, suffer loss) the loss of all things, and count them but rubbish (cow dung) so that I may gain Christ, and may be found in Him, not having a righteousness of my own derived from the Law, but that which is through faith in Christ, the righteousness which comes from God on the basis of faith, that I may know Him and the power of His resurrection and the fellowship (have in common) of His sufferings (something undergone, that is, hardship or pain; an emotion or influence affection, affliction, motion, suffering.):, being conformed (to assimilate:) to render like to His death; in order that I may attain (to meet against, that is, arrive at) to the resurrection from the dead;*
> ~Philippians 3:8-10 addition mine with Strong's)

Many people around the world in various churches practice self-flagellation (practice of mortification (a feeling of humiliation or shame, as through some injury to one's pride or self-respect, a cause or source of such humiliation or shame, the practice of asceticism by penitential discipline to overcome desire for sin and to strengthen the will.), of the flesh. (Definitions from Dictionary.com)

Prior to Jesus dying on the cross, He experienced flagellation in our place with a cat of nine tails (leather straps with bits of bone, rock and metal). He was given 39 stripes on his back (some say the number of known diseases at the time) in which His suffering (the suffering Messiah) was reflected in Isaiah 53:5.

*"But He was wounded for our transgressions, He was bruised for our guilt and iniquities; the chastisement {needful to obtain} pace and well-being was upon Him, and the stripes [that wounded] Him we ae healed and made whole (by His stripes we are healed)."*
~Isaiah 53:5 (AMP) addition mine

Jesus paid the price by suffering with suffering by being beaten to a bloody pulp, being physically abused with punches to the face, mocked with a crown of thorns pushed down into his brow prior to being crucified and then having wooden nails/spikes driven in His hands (wrists) and feet, refused drink (given vinegar when He was thirsty) and then having died, had a spear driven into His side as water (most likely the sac around the heart filled with fluid) poured forth. He did all of this so we would not have to suffer like He did for us in our place.

I believe that this suffering that we are told to have, the fellowship of suffering, is not us suffering (of course we will with the world against us) or imitating His suffering with self-flagellation so somehow we will gain the resurrection of the dead. I believe that the suffering that we identify with is His suffering on the cross in our place.

*"I have been crucified with Christ (a past event that took place, not us physical on the cross before or after the event on Calvary), and it is no longer I who live, but (in contrast) Christ lives in me, and the life which I now live (physically live in my human flesh), I live by faith in the Son of God (and His work that He did on the cross and His resurrection), who loved me (His motivation) and gave Himself up for me (so I would not have to go through the physical pain of suffering with self-flagellation)."*
~Galatians 2:20 addition mine

Paul again identified with this death on the cross in I Corinthians 15:30-31.

> *"Why are we also in danger every hour (suffering)? I affirm, brethren, by the boasting in which I have in Christ Jesus (who suffered on the cross), I die daily (I identify with the death on the cross by dying to my flesh, dying to my will and living unto His will."*
> ~I Corinthians 15:30-31 addition mine

This is what Paul is talking about when he says, "the fellowship (having in common) of His sufferings (the cross).

Is there a suffering according to the will of God? Most definitely.

> *"Beloved, do not be surprised at the fiery ordeal among you, which comes upon you for your testing, a something strange thing were happening to you:"* ~
> I Peter 4:12

There are ordeals that we suffer and they are part of testing in or lives.

> *"But to the degree that you share the suffering of Christ (the fellowship, common sufferings), keep on rejoicing, so that also at the revelation of His glory (when He returns a second time) you may rejoice with exultation."*
> ~I Peter 4:13 addition mine

> *"If you are reviled for the name of Christ, you are blessed because the Spirit of glory and of God rests on you."*
> ~I Peter 4:14

Peter spoke of this suffering at the hands of unreasonable people. Jesus like His Father gives us an example to follow when suffering unjustly. We saw that;

> *"God demonstrates His own love towards us in that while we

*were yet, sinners, Christ (Jesus) died for us (suffered on the cross)."*
~Romans 5:8

*"Servants, be submissive to your master with all respect, not only to those who are good and gentle, but also to those who are unreasonable. For this finds favor if for the sake of conscience toward God a person bears up under sorrows (to experience a sensation or impression (usually painful) when suffering unjustly (wrongfully)."*
~I Peter 2:19 addition mine

Being able to yield your will under unjust people is an act of worship as you trust God in all things.

*"For what credit is there if when you sin and are harshly treated, (suffering) you endure it (bear up) with patience? But (in contrast when you do what is right and suffer for it you patiently endure it, this finds favor with God."*
~I Peter 2:20 addition mine

Again, we see that there is suffering for the believer. We will later go forward to I Peter 4 and see what it means to suffer in the will of God. But for now let us continue to see the example by Jesus how to suffer properly.

*"For you have been called for this purpose, since Christ also suffered for you, leaving you an example for you to follow in His steps."*
~I Peter 2:21

Many people wonder for years what their calling and purpose is when they become Christians. Whatever it is, part of that calling and purpose is to suffer like Christ suffered for you. He was kind enough to leave us an example, so we would not have to guess what this suffering entails.

*"Who committed no sin, nor was there any deceit found in His mouth, and while being reviled, He did not revile in return, while*

*suffering, He uttered no threats, but kept entrusting Himself to Him who judges righteously."*

~I Peter 2:22-23

When we suffer and we revile with deceit in our mouth and utter threats while suffering we are in essence not entrusting (put trust) in our God who will deal with the unreasonable people in our lives.

Now there is a suffering that is the will of Christ, and there is a suffering that is not the will of Christ. The problem arises when we embrace the suffering that is not the will of Christ thinking that it will somehow make us worthy and that somehow by suffering we are knowing the "power of His resurrection and the fellowship of His sufferings" by conforming to His death. (Philippians 3:10)

*"Therefore those also who suffer according to the will of God shall entrust their souls to the faithful Creator in doing what is right."*

~I Peter 4:19

Like we saw in I Peter 2:23, Jesus suffered by not retaliating verbally in His suffering because He entrusted (trusted) that God was in control, so it is when we suffer according to the will of God will entrust (trust) God, and we can do what is right and not what is wrong.

So what is this suffering that we are to suffer according to the will of God all about?

*"If you are reviled for the name of Christ (not just because of generalized suffering), you are blessed because the Spirit of glory and of God rests on you (in your suffering). Make sure that none of you suffers as a murderer, or thief or evildoer, or a troublesome meddler (self-inflicted suffering) but (in contrast to that type of suffering) if anyone suffers as a Christian (like Paul and the other apostles suffered and even a Jesus suffered), he is not to be ashamed, but is to glorify God in this name."*

~I Peter 14-16 addition mine

To "know of the power of His resurrection" and to know the

fellowship (have in common) of His sufferings (not just the cross, but the rejection and mocking) and to be conformed (identify with) His death, we must suffer.

To live the maximized, overcoming, more than conqueror, victorious, blessed, abundant, successful and prosperous lifestyle, we will have to endure the suffering as we identify with what Christ went through on the road to the cross. The way Christ Jesus dealt with the suffering is found in Hebrews 12:2.

> *"Fixing our eyes on Jesus, the author and finisher of our faith, who for the joy set before Him endured the cross (death for him, identification of death for us), despising the shame (no one said suffering was not pleasant), and has sat down at the right hand of the throne of God."*

# CHAPTER TWENTY

## THE HELPING THE POOR PRINCIPLE

In our quest to gain wealth, we tend to forget those who are poor and need our help. Sometimes we tend to look down on them and feel superior because we have risen above poverty and declare that if we did it, then they can do it. Sometimes we label people who are poor and suffering through trials, troubles and tribulations.

Remember that one of the richest and wealthiest men at one time, Andrew Carnegie wrote a pamphlet called *The Gospel of Wealth*.

Some people assume that simply giving to the poor or doing other acts of charity will ensure them a place in heaven. Their works and good deeds become merit badges or their get out of hell free pass. Jesus was very clear on how to get into the presence of the Father, and it was not by good works/deeds. As seen in the previous chapter, and I believe it bears repeating and is not just redundant, Paul stated;

> *"Finally, my brethren, rejoice in the Lord. To write the same things again is no trouble to me, and it is a safeguard for you."*
> ~Philippians 3:1

Consider this a safeguard against wealth/money/riches having you instead of you being in control of the wealth/money/riches.

> *"Jesus told him, "I am the way, the truth, and the life. No one comes to the Father except through me."*
> ~John 14:6

Some people feel that they are excused from taking care of the poor.

They point to Jesus' statement when a very expensive nard/ointment was used by breaking an alabaster box (which also was not cheap), and poured over his feet by a woman and wiped up with her hair.

> *"Mary then took a pound of very costly perfume of pure nard, and anointed the feet of Jesus and wiped His feet with her hair; and the house was filled with the fragrance of the perfume. But Judas Iscariot, one of His disciples, who was intending to betray Him, said, "Why was this perfume not sold for three hundred denarii and given to poor people? Now he said this, not because he was concerned about the poor, but because he was a thief, and as he had the money box, he used to pilfer what was put into it."*
>
> ~John 12:3-7

Jesus' response (and our excuse) was,

> *"Therefore Jesus said, "Let her alone, so that she may keep it for the day of My burial. "For you always have the poor with you, but you do not always have Me."*
>
> ~John 12:7-8

Since even Jesus believed that we will always have the poor with us so we don't need to take care of the poor with our hard earned money, right? No, when Judas was thinking only about the loss of money for him, Jesus spoke into that moment in time, that we would always have the poor with us. There would be many more opportunities to give to the poor after He was crucified, dead, buried, and risen from the dead and returned back to the Father.

Here are just a few verses found in the book of Positive Action (Pro-Verbs) concerning the poor. There are many poor throughout the Bible.

> *"Speak up for those who cannot speak for themselves, for the rights of all who are destitute. Speak up and judge fairly; defend the rights of the poor and needy."*
>
> ~Proverbs 31:8

*"Do not exploit the poor because they are poor and do not crush the needy in court, for the Lord will take up their case and will exact life for life."*

*~Proverbs 22:22-23*

*"Do not withhold good from those to whom it is due, when it is in your power to act. Do not say to your neighbor, "Come back tomorrow and I'll give it to you"—when you already have it with you."*

*~Proverbs 3:27-28*

*"A generous person will prosper; whoever refreshes others will be refreshed."*

*~Proverbs 11:25*

*"It is a sin to despise one's neighbor, but blessed is the one who is kind to the needy."*

*~Proverbs 14:21*

*"Whoever oppresses the poor shows contempt for their Maker, but whoever is kind to the needy honors God.*

*~Proverbs 14:31*

*"Whoever is kind to the poor lends to the Lord, and he will reward them for what they have done."*

*~Proverbs 19:17*

*"The generous will themselves be blessed, for they share their food with the poor."*

*~Proverbs 22:9*

*"Those who give to the poor will lack nothing, but those who close their eyes to them receive many curses."*

*~Proverbs 28:27*

Many "positive thinkers" believe that what Andrew Carnegie spoke and did is true, and this principle will work for anyone, but when Jesus is Lord (kurios, the one in control) it is key to being a true Christian.

## CHAPTER TWENTY-ONE

## THE DREAMS, DESIRES, GOALS, VISION PRINCIPLE

*"Delight yourself in the Lord and He will give you the desires of your heart."*

~Psalm 37:4

There are many non-Christians and Christians alike who have employed this principle and had great success doing it. Many times Christian's poo-poo those who have utilized their imaginations and refuse to dream dreams and believe that their dreams can be a God thing in their lives.

I like the term coined by the Disney Corporation to describe the thinkers in their employment. They are called, *Imagineers*. When you look back through history you will see people who have ideas and actually acted on those ideas to better planet Earth and mankind. Of course, there are those who do not give credit for their imaginations and take credit for their own wonderfulness. This is called humanism, where humans think they are gods to be worshipped.

There is "nothing new under the sun"—that is unless you are a "new creation" under the Son. (Ecclesiastes 1:9, II Corinthians 5:17) Early Imagineers/positive thinkers/humanists are found in the book of beginnings (Genesis) in the land of Shinar. Here is the chronological order of their story found in Genesis 10:32 and Genesis 11:1-9.

1. After the flood, the nations (birth out of the ark) were separated on the earth.
2. The whole earth used the same language and the same words. NOTE: As a Speech-Language Pathologist, I find this event fascinating.

3. They said, (communicated with one another) to one another, "come, let us make bricks and burn them thoroughly."
4. They used brick for stone and they used tar for mortar. NOTE: They used man made substituted materials for God's provision in the building of the tower of Babel.
5. They said (communicated with one another), "come let us, build for ourselves a city, and tower whose top will reach into the heaven, and let us make for ourselves a name, *otherwise we will be scattered abroad over the face of the whole earth*. NOTE: They will soon find out that the Job principle will be taking effect in their lives as "what I feared has come upon me." (Job 3:25)
6. The Lord came down to see the city and the tower which the sons of men had built.
7. The Lord said, 'Behold they are one people (humans) and they all have the same language' (language= an agreed upon code used to communicate).
8. This is how they began to do (building a tower in an attempt to make a name for themselves and not for God), and now nothing which they purpose to do will be impossible for them. NOTE: This still holds true today among those who do not acknowledge God. Positive mental humanist still declare "if you can conceive it you can achieve it." NOTE: Those submitted to the Lordship of Jesus declare, "Believe it, Receive it, Do it." The difference is the conception (conceive) of the thought is not from man's own imagination but from God Himself.
9. Come, let Us (the same Us found in Genesis 1:26) go down and there confuse their language, that they may not understand one another's speech.
10. So, the Lord scattered them abroad from there over the face of the whole earth; and they stopped building the city (their dreams and imaginations). NOTE: What they were attempting to do ended up being exactly what they feared, being scattered.
11. Therefore (in reference to what 1-10 said) its name was called

Babel, because there the Lord confused the language of the whole earth, and from there the Lord scattered them abroad over the face of the earth. NOTE: They were trying to make a name for themselves and because of their humanistic reasonings they made a name, the name of Bable (confusing language).

Up to this point, this thing called imagination has been presented in a negative light. But we will begin to see that imagination is a good thing, especially when the imagination is captured and submitted to the Lordship of Jesus.

God's heartbeat is for us to have dreams, desires, visions, and imaginations (captive and submitted to Him).

> *"Casting down imaginations, and every high thing that exalts itself against the knowledge of God, and bringing into captivity every thought to the obedience of Christ; and having in a readiness to revenge all disobedience, when your obedience is fulfilled."*
> *~II Corinthians 10:5-6*

The imaginations being cast down are not godly imaginations, they are ungodly imaginations, imaginations of the flesh and the d-evil. Adam and Eve had God-imaginations in the garden. God planted them there from the beginning. The d-evil crept into the Garden and the first temptation was an attack on the thoughts that God placed in Adam and Eve's mind. The first tactic against God's thoughts was to plant the seed of doubt into their minds.

"…indeed has God said, 'You shall not eat from any tree of the garden?" (Genesis 3:1) The second wave of attack was an attack on the consequences of disobedience which was that you shall die. The d-evil said, "you shall surely not die." (Genesis 3:4) The third wave of imagination attach from the d-evil was against God's reasoning to hold out on her, "for God knows that in the day you eat from it your eyes will be opened, and you will be like God, knowing good and evil." (Genesis 3:5)

God had planted dreams and visions and gave them a purpose. He also gave them dominion and authority to deal with "every living thing that creeps on the earth." (Genesis 1:26) In Genesis A & E were to cast down imaginations placed in their minds by the d-evil and to bring into captivity every thought that the d-evil placed in their minds. We are to take imaginations that exalt themselves above God and bring those imaginations into obedience. What was lost in disobedience was to be brought into obedience. Fulfilled obedience revenges disobedience. (I Corinthians 10:6)

*"Where there is no vision, the people cast off restraint; but blessed is he who keeps the Law."*
~Pro-Verbs 29:18

*"Where there is no vision [no redemptive revelation of God], the people perish; but he who keeps the [law of God, which includes that of man]—blessed (happy, fortunate, and enviable) is he."*
~Pro-Verbs 28:18 (AMP)

Other meanings for "the people perish" includes
- people cast off restraint
- they run wild
- people are unrestrained
- law and order disappear
- is a nation without order
- people run wild
- people abandon restraint
- a people is breached
- no interpreter to a sinful nation
- the people shall be scattered abroad
- people made naked

In contrast to all of these negative things, we see that when we have a revelatory vision (God's imagination) we are happy, to be envied and blessed.

## GOD-GIVEN DESIRES

*"Delight yourself in the Lord and He will give you the desires of your heart."*
~Psalm 37:4

**DELIGHT:** (*aw-nag'*)=A primitive root; to be *soft* or pliable, that is, (figuratively) *effeminate* or luxurious: - delicate (-ness), (have) delight (self), sport self.

NOTE: Delight is a verb that does not mean to be giddy but to be soft and pliable to yield your will to Him.

**GIVE:** nâthan (*naw-than'*)=A primitive root; to *give*, used with great latitude of application (*put, make*, etc.): - add, apply, appoint, ascribe, assign, X avenge, X be ([healed]), bestow, bring (forth, hither), cast, cause, charge, come, commit consider, count, + cry, deliver (up), direct, distribute do, X doubtless, X without fail, fasten, frame, X get, give (forth, over, up), grant, hang (up), X have, X indeed, lay (unto charge, up), (give) leave, lend, let (out), + lie, lift up, make, + O that, occupy, offer, ordain, pay, perform, place, pour, print, X pull, put (forth), recompense, render, requite, restore, send (out), set (forth), shew, shoot forth (up). + sing, + slander, strike, [sub-] mit, suffer, X surely, X take, thrust, trade, turn, utter, + weep, X willingly, + withdraw, + would (to) God, yield.

NOTE: I believe this given to us by God means to place within us and to bring that which is placed to pass. So it is with imaginations that we have within us; when we act by faith and actions then those things will happen.

**DESIRES:** mish'âlâh (*mish-aw-law'*)=From H7592; a *request*: - desire, petition. H7592: shâ'al shâ'êl=*(shaw-al', shaw-ale')*=A primitive root; to *inquire*; by implication to *request*; by extension to *demand*: - ask (counsel, on), beg, borrow, lay to charge, consult, demand, desire, X earnestly, enquire, + greet, obtain leave, lend, pray, request, require, + salute, X straitly, X surely, wish.

NOTE: Wishes, dreams, imaginations are when God pulls aside the curtain of our minds, and we can see God things.

**HEART:** lêb (*labe*)=A form of H3824; the *heart*; also used (figuratively) very widely for the feelings, the will and even the intellect; likewise for the *centre* of anything: - + care for, comfortably, consent, X considered, courag [-eous], friend [-ly], ([broken-], [hard-], [merry-], [stiff-], [stout-], double) heart ([-ed]), X heed, X I, kindly, midst, mind (-ed), X regard ([-ed)], X themselves, X unawares, understanding, X well, willingly, wisdom. H3824: lêbâb (*lay-bawb'*) From H3823; the *heart* (as the most interior organ); used also like H3820: - + bethink themselves, breast, comfortably, courage, ([faint], [tender-] H3823: lâbab (*law-bab'*)=A primitive root; properly to *be enclosed* (as if with *fat*); by implication (as denominative from H3824) to *unheart*, that is, (in a good sense) *transport* (with love), or (in a bad sense) *stultify*; also (as denominative from H3834) to *make cakes:* - make cakes, ravish, be wise.

NOTE: The heart is more than just the physical blood pump, but it is the core, our human spirit, the center, the heartbeat of our passions and desires. The Word says;

> *"The spirit of man is the lamp of the Lord."*
> ~Pro-Verb 20:27

You have the human spirit (little /s/ locate inside your body) which is inhabited by the Big S (the Holy Spirit), Christ (the Anointed One) who is in you and is our hope of glory. (Colossians 1:27). This place is where the fruit grows, and the gifts flow; where there is revelation, wisdom, service takes place, intimacy with God, and the location for the communication system between you and God.

I believe that the spirit/heart is the place where imagination takes place and that as our thoughts, our brain receives the imaginations from God, the perception is in the spirit.

We are an intricate being of a spirit (the lamp of the Lord), the soul (our minds/thoughts, will/choice maker), and our physical body where the soul and spirit are housed. (I Thessalonians 5:23)

The d-evil can also place in imaginations (evil ones) that we must take authority over. We must develop a renewed mindset where we set our minds on the Spirit and not on the flesh.

# CHAPTER TWENTY-TWO

## THE DISCIPLINE WITH PURPOSE PRINCIPLE

*"...on the other hand, discipline yourself for the purpose of godliness;"*
~I Timothy 4:7

*"But solid food/meat is for the mature, who because of practice have their senses trained to discern food and evil."*
~Hebrews 5:14

DISCIPLINE/EXERCISE: gumnazō (*goom-nad'-zo*)=From G1131; to *practice naked* (in the games), that is, *train* (figuratively): - exercise. G1131: gumnos (*goom-nos'*)=Of uncertain affinity; *nude* (absolutely or relatively, literally or figuratively): - naked.

One of the principles/laws of success is "discipline/exercise." If you don't discipline yourself/exercise/practice yourself you will remain weak and flabby. This is true in business, your physical being, your spiritual growth. You must have a goal and do the things that you need to do to accomplish that goal.

The condition of the world and the world to come in the future was bleak. The Holy Spirit was speaking and not in generalities. But the Spirit (Holy) explicitly says in I Timothy1-7

1. In later times some will fall away from the faith.
2. Paying attention to deceitful spirits and doctrines of demons.
3. By means of the hypocrisy of liars seared in their own conscience as with a branding iron.
4. Men who forbid marriage and advocate abstaining from foods which God has created to be gratefully shared in by those who

believe and know the truth
5. Worldly fables fit only for old women.

## ON THE OTHER HAND
*"...on the other hand (compared to I Timothy 4:1-7) discipline yourself for the purpose of godliness."*

~I Timothy 4:7

The word discipline means to practice naked. In the days of the games in Greece the competitors did not just show up and run a race—they practiced and exercised in preparations for the games. In those days they would wear long tunics that would tangle up around their legs and trip them up, so they would disrobe. Now, they may have kept on clothes covering their private parts, but they may have gone totally naked to be unencumbered. In the book of Hebrews we see this concept mentioned again. The writer of Hebrews (whoever that was) had just written about men and women of faith in what is known as "The Hall of Faith." Hebrews chapter 12 word, *Therefore*.

## GOING FROM MILK TO MEAT BY DISCIPLINE/EXERCISE
Sometimes in the mundane routine of life, we get in a rut and become dull of hearing. We become accustomed to milk for babies and not meat for mature beings.

*"For everyone who partakes only of milk is not accustomed to the word of righteousness for he is an infant. But solid food/meat is for the mature, who because of practice/exercise/discipline have their senses trained to discern good and evil."*

~Hebrews 5:13, 14

I believe that when we practice/exercise/discipline ourselves by the Word of God we go from getting wisdom to also getting understanding in how our world works.

*"Wisdom is the principle thing; therefore, get wisdom and in all*

*thy getting, get understanding."*

~Pro-Verbs 4:7

*"The beginning of wisdom is: Acquire wisdom; and with all your acquiring get understanding."*

~Pro-Verbs 4:7

*"Therefore, since we have so great a cloud of witnesses (those mention in the Hall of Faith) surrounding us, let us also lay aside every encumbrance and the sin which so easily entangles us, and let us run with endurance the race that is set before us, fixing our eyes on Jesus, the author and the finisher of faith, who for the joy set before Him endured the cross, despising the shame and has sat down at the right hand of the throne of God."*

~Hebrews 12:1-2

Notice that "the sin" is singular, not "sins" like a lot of sinning in multiple ways. While that may be true, the root of sins (plural) is one sin, unbelief.

*"Take care brethren, that there may to be in any one of you an evil, unbelieving heart that falls away from the living God."*

~Hebrews 3:12

*"for bodily discipline is only of little profit, but (in contrast to) godliness is profitable for all things since it holds promise for (1) the present life (2) and also for the life to come."*

~I Timothy 4:8 addition mine

This does not say that bodily exercise is useless but compared to spiritual exercise/discipline there is no comparison. Bodily exercise is for earth, but spiritual discipline is for earth and heaven.

As stated in the introduction, I believe these principles/laws will work for the non-believer but especially for the True Believer.

*"It is a trustworthy statement deserving full acceptance. For it*

*for this we labor and strive, because we have fixed our hope on the living God, who is the Savior of ALL men (including men, wo-men and hu-mans) ESPECIALLY OF BELIEVERS."*
~I Timothy 4:9-10 addition mine

Paul prescribed (like a medicine) and taught (passed on the information to others) these things. I believe that these things are fivefold found in I Timothy 4:12. It is for young and old, but don't let anyone look down on your youth (at the time Timothy was around 30 years old).

## FIVE AREAS TO DISCIPLINE YOURSELF IN FOR THE PURPOSE OF GOD

1. Speech: What we say. What we confess (say the same thing that God says via the Word, (Romans 4:17, Romans 10:8-10)
2. Conduct: How we act. "Faith without corresponding actions is of none effect." (James 2:17)
3. Love: What motivates us: Why do we do the things we do? (2 Corinthians 5:14-15, John 14:21)
4. Faith: What we believe (trust in, cling to, rely on, adhere to, cleave to) (Hebrews 11:1, 2 Corinthians 5:7, Hebrews 11:6)
5. Purity: Our character manifested when no one is watching. Galatians 5:22-26)

We are to show ourselves as an example of someone who believes.

## THE WORD AND DISCIPLINING YOURSELF FOR THE PURPOSE OF GODLINESS

1. Give attention to the public reading of Scripture
2. Give attention to exhortation
3. Give attention to teaching
4. Do not neglect the spiritual gift within you which was bestowed on you through prophetic utterance with the laying on of hands by the presbytery.
5. Take pains with these things.
6. Be absorbed in them so your progress will be evident.
7. Pay close attention to yourself and to your teaching.

8. Persevere in these things.

*"...for as you do this you will ensure salvation both for yourself and for those who hear you."*
~I Timothy 4:16

In my mind, doing these things will take discipline with a purpose.

# CHAPTER TWENTY-THREE

## THE WILL ON EARTH PRINCIPLE

*"Thy (Father God) Kingdom (rule, reign, foundation of power) come (from headquarters [heaven] down to the outpost [earth] Thy (Father God) will (wish/desire) be done (accomplished and manifested) on earth (the outpost) AS IT IS in heaven (headquarters)."*
~Matthew 6:10 addition mine

To live the lifestyle that you desire you must develop your Kingdom Thinking. So often we think like the d-evil with a defeatist attitude. One of the most common ways is to think that just because something happens in our lives, that must be the will of God. This thinking has infiltrated our prayer life as we pray to God and tack on; "Thy will be done" or "If it be Thy will." We think of God sitting up in heaven and distributing out His will and to not accept it makes us look like we are in control. *If* we get sick we accept that sickness is the will of God, and *if* He wants us to be well, then He will force His will on us.

*"Thy (Father God) will (wish, desire) be done (accomplished/manifested) on earth (where there is sin, sickness, dis-ease, dis-comfort, dis-stress, dys-function) AS IT IS (just like it is, the mirror image) in heaven (where there is forgiveness and deliverance, healing, ease, comfort, no stress, and function)."*
Matthew 6:10 (emphasis and addition mine, Ruminator Style

How silly is it to just accept what we already have on earth is what is in heaven. *If* the will of God is already happening on earth, why even pray since it is already here. *If* the will of God is, for example, sickness, then we should never pray for healing as that would place us out of the will of God.

We might as well pray, "The d-evil's will be done on earth as it is in hell, if it be Thy will to be done."

I know for a fact that it is *not* God's will for anyone to perish, but people do perish every day because they choose the will of the d-evil (to die and go to hell or to be sick and die) over the will of God to be saved.

> *"The Lord is not slow about His promise, as some count slowness, but is patient toward you, not wishing for any to perish but for all to come to repentance."*
>
> ~2 Peter 3:9

Don't get mc wrong, I am not against laying down your plans before the Lord and asking for His will to take place, but we are not called to just accept whatever comes down the pike as the will of God. I call that *Doris Day Faith,* walking through life singing whatever will be; Que sera. We act like God is on the mountain top like a Greek or Roman God who is randomly throwing down lightning bolts, striking whosoever gets hit with a good, bad, or ugly bomb. We are like the centerpiece in a chess match between God and the d-evil and sometimes it looks like God is losing. We act as if God's will is a roll of the cosmic dice, and we will either get a 7 or 11 or we roll snake-eyes. Sometime we act as if God is some Hindu deity and whatever happens to us is how it is and will be the rest of our lives as we live in our caste system. Oops a fly landed on us, better not brush it off, it could be Uncle Raheesh. Or His will is based on good or bad luck or a bad case of karma.

No, we need to read His Word, pray, and ask for wisdom so we can know that we know that we know what the will of God is and act on the Word.

# CHAPTER TWENTY-FOUR

## THE STRENGTH AND SUPPLY PRINCIPLE

In a world where there is weakness and lack/poverty, we need this principle to survive. In 2020 and into 2021 we are going through *The Pandemic Of Fear* ruled by *Systemic Sin*. Our world is filled with riots, political unrest, anarchy, looting, brutal bullies, B.L.M (Black Lives Matter), ANTIFA (a political hate group), various white (K.K.K.) and black (Black Panthers) supremacy groups.

In these dazes of Systemic Fear fueled by Systemic Sin (not just systemic racism) manifested by Systemic Hate with the Systemic Root of Bitterness wrapped around the minds and hearts of humanity, there is a need for strength, supply, love *of another kind* (as Amy Grant sang).

> *"This Book of the Law shall not depart out of your mouth but you shall meditate on it day and night that you may observe and do according to all that is written in it. For then you shall make your way prosperous and then have good success."*
> ~Joshua 1:8 (AMP

> *"Have I not commanded you? Be strong, vigorous, and courageous. Be not afraid, neither be dismayed, for the Lord is with you wherever you go."*
> ~Joshua 1:9 (AMP)

> *"I have strength for all things in Christ Who empowers me (I am ready for anything and equal to anything through Him Who infuses inner strength into me: I am self-sufficient in Christ's sufficiency."*
> ~Philippians 4:13 (AMP)

> *"And my God will liberally supply (fill to the full) your every need according to His riches in glory in Christ Jesus."*
> ~Philippians 4:19 (AMP)

I believe that the Principle of Strength and Supply is found in *The Secret*. I am not talking about the metaphysical book of the same title but the spiritual, Holy Ghost-inspired principle. Paul had written to the Church in Philippi an epistle/letter (remember the epistle is not the wife of an apostle but a letter). In Philippians 4:13 we see that "I can do all things through Christ who strengthens me" and then in Philippian 4:19, "my God shall supply all your needs according to His riches in glory in Christ Jesus." The Secret is the principles that is talking about finances, but I believe it can apply to anything in your life and your faith walk.

Previously in chapter four of Philippians, Paul shared to not be anxious and how to have the peace of God guarding our hearts and minds in Christ Jesus, because that is where the attacks come to bring you down and not fulfilling your full potential, your purpose in life and your destiny. Learning these principles will be the keys to unlock *The Secret* and power of *Supply* and *Strength*.

The first think you must have to access *The Secret* is have a *can do attitude*. The old saying is, "Can't never did anything."

CAN DO: ischuō (is-khoo'-o)=From G2479; to have (or exercise) force (literally or figuratively): - beable, avail, can do ([-not]), could, be good, might, prevail, be of strength, be whole, + much work.

By your choice, your volition, your free will you have to determine to *do* what you have to *do*. As a True Believer you have a *force* within you that gives you the ability to avail/prevail. You have *mighty* in you to accomplish *all* things. You are whole and able to do much work in your life. The d-evil is doing everything he can to make you anxious and worried that you *can't do* anything. (We will earn more in the principle of imagination).

Another key to *The Secret* is to realize that you are *weak* and in yourself you cannot do anything, however you have *strength* to do *all* things when His grace is in play. His *power* is perfected.

STRENGTH: plēroō (play-ro'-o)=From G4134; to make replete, that is, (literally) to cram (a net), level up (a hollow), or (figuratively) to furnish (or imbue, diffuse, influence), satisfy, execute (an office), finish (a period or task), verify (or coincide with a prediction), etc.: - accomplish, X after, (be) complete, end, expire, fill (up), fulfil, (be, make) full (come), fully preach, perfect, supply. G4134: plērēs (play'-race) From G4130; replete, or covered over; by analogy complete: - full. 4130: plēthō (play'-tho, pleh'-o,)=A prolonged form of a primary word pleō (which appears only as an alternate in certain tenses and in the reduplicated form of pimplēmi to "fill" (literally or figuratively [imbue, influence, supply]); specifically to fulfil (time): - accomplish, full (. . . come), furnish.

> *"I have strength for all things in Christ Who empowers me [I am ready for anything and equal to anything] through Him Who infuses inner strength into me; I am self-sufficient in Christ's sufficiency."*
> ~Philippians 4:13 (AMP)

When the attack by the d-evil is on, his goal is to deplete you of strength and convince you that you are weak, so why even try? Jesus came to make you replete with strength. The d-evil will send a messenger (d-evil angels) and weaken you and convince you that it is not God's will for you to be strong. (2 Corinthians 12:7-10) As you walk by *faith* and not by *sight* or things revealed to the senses (sight, sound, smell, touch, taste, equilibrium (balance) and proprioception (awareness of your surroundings) you *must* realize that in your *weakness* that His *Power Of Christ* is being perfected. So by *faith*,

> *"...let the weak say I am strong."*
> ~Joel 3:10

The power of Christ (The Anointed One) is the power (duNAMis, dynamic miraculous, dynamite) of The Anointed One with His yoke breaking, burden lifting, oppression removing, healing power of the Holy Ghost that gives you strength to do all things in the Anointing.

The next part of unlocking *The Secret* is realizing that poverty is *not* the will of God in your life, but liberal supply is.

SUPPLY: plēroō (play-ro'-o)=From G4134; to make replete, that is, (literally) to cram (a net), level up (a hollow), or (figuratively) to furnish (or imbue, diffuse, influence), satisfy, execute (an office), finish (a period or task), verify (or coincide with a prediction), etc.: - accomplish, X after, (be) complete, end, expire, fill (up), fulfil, (be, make) full (come), fully preach, perfect, supply. G4134: plērēs (play'-race)=From G4130; replete, or covered over; by analogy complete: - full. G4134:plēthō (play'-tho, pleh'-o,)=A prolonged form of a primary word pleō (which appears only as an alternate in certain tenses and in the reduplicated form of pimplēmi to "fill" (literally or figuratively [imbue, influence, supply]); specifically to fulfil (time): - accomplish, full (... come), furnish.

> *"And my God will liberally* supply *(fill to the full) your every need (not your greed) according to His riches in glory in Christ Jesus."*
> ~Philippians 4:19 (AMP with emphasis and addition mine)

The d-evil is doing everything he can to convince you that you are called to poverty, lack, need. The d-evil will do everything he can to make you believe that God does not have enough to meet your needs because His riches in glory in Christ Jesus is depleted. God's economy is not like the world's economy. We must unlock *The Secret*; we must understand *The Mystery*.

God's heartbeat for us is to have wisdom and understanding of *The Secret* and *Mysteries Of God*.

> *"...we speak wisdom among those who are mature; a wisdom in a mystery, the hidden wisdom which God predestined before the ages to our glory; the wisdom which none of the rulers of this age has understood; for if they had understood it they would not have crucified the Lord of glory; but just as it is written (in Isaiah 64:4, Isaiah 65:17) things which eye has not seen and ear has*

*not heard and which have not entered the heart of man, all the God has prepared for those who love Him for to us* god revealed them *through the Spirit/from the Spirit searches all things even the depths of God."*
~I Corinthians 2:7-9 emphasis mine

*"The* secret *things belong to the Lord our God, but the things* revealed *belong to us and to our sons forever, that we may observe all the words of this Law (principles)."*
~Deuteronomy 29:29 addition mine

I believe and try to live out the revealed things and as I am obedient to the revealed things more will be revealed. God has revealed to us the secret of *strength* and *supply* in *The Secret*. Once again, the metaphysical book got it partially correct as they identified *The Secret* as the Law of Attraction). They state that if you would just be positive and not be negative that you will attract positive things in your life including material things. The flip side of the metaphysical secret is that you will attract negative things and people in your life so we must change our way of thinking, speaking and doing. I believe that is a God-principle but without Jesus as Lord and our minds being renewed based on the Word of God and speaking the Word with a renewed mind and doing things by acting by faith, then we implode and things will eventually fall apart.

## THE SECRET

MYSTERY/HIDDEN/SECRET: apokruptō (ap-ok-roop'-to)=- From G575 and G2928; to conceal away (that is, fully); figuratively to keep secret: - hide.

Paul rejoiced that the church in Philippi had revived their concern for him by sending him money. *The Secret* is about money but more about provision. Paul knew they were concerned and knew that they lacked an opportunity. Let's look at *The Secret*.

Paul did not *speak* from a place of want. He did not deny want but did not speak from a position of want. Paul did not deny reality.

He was in prison, he had needs, he did suffer, but he did not speak from the position of need/want. Why? He knew who his strength and supply came from, and it was not the church in Philippi.

David sang, "The Lord is my Shepherd I shall not *want*." (Psalm 23:1) I'm thinking that if I am wanting, then I may need to check out my relationship with the Shepherd.

WANT: husterēsis (hoos-ter'-ay-sis)=From G5302; a falling short, that is, (specifically) penury: - want. G5302: hustereō (hoos-ter-eh'-o)=From G5306; to be later, that is, (by implication) to be inferior; genitively to fall short (be deficient): - come behind (short), be destitute, fall, lack, suffer need, (be in) want, be the worse. G5306: hupo (hoop-o')=A primary preposition; under, that is, (with the genitive) of place (beneath), or with verbs (the agency or means, through); (with the accusative) of place (whither [underneath] or where [below]) or time (when [at]): - among, by, from, in, of, under, with. In compounds it retains the same genitive applications, especially of inferior position or condition, and specifically covertly or moderately.

Paul did just not automatically learn how to *speak*. Paul learned how to be *content* and exercised contentment until it becomes second nature. Paul learned *contentment*. The contentment that Paul learned was not just to be content/satisfied in the good times but also in the bad and ugly times, in *whatever circumstances* he was in whether it was surrounded by fellow believers or in chains in a prison.

CONTENTMENT: autarkēs (ow-tar'-kace)= self-complacent, that is, contented: - content.

WHATEVER: no matter what *circumstances/state*: (1) a condition, detail, part, or attribute, with respect to time, place, manner, agent, etc., that accompanies, determines, or modifies a fact or event; a modifying or influencing factor (2) the existing conditions or state of affairs surrounding and affecting an agent (3) the condition or state of a person with respect to income and material welfare.

NOTE: You may have heard the phrase, "I am *in* trouble" or "I'm *in* a fix" or "I'm *in* a good place" or "I am *in Christ*." Being *in* something speaks of a position that can be good, bad, or ugly. How you speak in the position that you are *in* will determine what happens in your life. Part of *The Secret* is learning how to *speak* in *whatever state* (good, bad or ugly) you find yourself *in*.

Paul gained knowledge of how to get along in life. This thing life is where you know how to operate in *The Secret*. In Philippians 4:12 Paul states I know how to:
- Get along with humble means
- How to live in prosperity
- How to live in *any* and *every* circumstance

Paul had learned *The Secret* of:
- Being filled
- Suffering need

When you have learned *The Secret* and you learned how to operate *The Secret* in whatever circumstances you are in, no matter if it is in humble means, in prosperity, in any and every circumstance, being filled and going hungry, both of having abundance and suffering need, then you can make the declaration that Paul made in prison:

"*I* can do *all things through Christ Who* strengthens me."
~Philippians 4:13 emphasis mine

*I have strength for all things in Christ Who empowers me [I am ready for anything and equal to anything through Him Who infuses inner strength into me; I am self-sufficient in Christ's sufficiency].*"
~Philippians 4:13 (AMP)

NOTE: Again, this strength is about finances and provision in finances, but I believe it can be applied in every area of our lives where we need to do something.

Now, with this knowledge of *The Secret* concerning how to "do all things through Christ who strengthens me," we can know that we know that we know, that your (my) God can and will *supply* all of your needs (not your greed) according to (on the basis of) His riches (not the worlds riches) in glory (in His presence) in Christ Jesus (in His anointing). This is how strength and supply can come to Paul *in* the middle of prisons where He can write the Word of God and praise and worship God at midnight with Silas.

> *"And my God will supply all your needs according to His riches in glory in Christ Jesus."*
> 
> ~Philippians 4:19

> *"And my god will liberally supply (fill to the full, , good measure, pressed down, overflowing) your every need according to His riches in glory (His presence) in Christ (the Anointed One and His anointing) Jesus (God is salvation)."*
> 
> ~Philippians 4:19 addition mine

## CHAPTER TWENTY-FIVE

## THE BENEFITS PACKAGE PRINCIPLE

*"Bless the Lord O my soul and all that is within me, bless His holy name. Bless the Lord, O my soul, and forget none of his benefits."*
~Psalm 103:1

NOTE: The word "benefits" is plural to imply there is more than just one. When you have a job, one of the things that you check on are the benefits.

BENEFITS: (1) something that is advantageous or good; an advantage (2) a payment or gift, as one made to help someone or given by an employer, an insurance company, or a public agency (3) an act of kindness; good deed; benefaction.

BENEFIT [Hebrew} gemûl (ghem-ool')=From H1580; treatment, that is, an act (of good or ill); by implication service or requital: - + as hast served, benefit, desert, deserving, that which he hath given, recompense, reward. H1508: gâmal (gaw-mal')=A primitive root; to treat a person (well or ill), that is, benefit or requite; by implication (of toil) to ripen, that is, (specifically) to wean: - bestow on, deal bountifully, do (good), recompense, requite, reward, ripen, + serve, wean, yield.

King David is the primary Psalmist in the book of Psalms.

"The variety of songs laments and praises in the book caused it to be left unnamed in the Old Testament. The Jews referred to it as

"The Book of Praises" while the LXX (The Greek Old Testament, or Septuagint; from the Latin: septuaginta, lit. 'seventy'; often abbreviated 70; in Roman numerals, LXX), is the earliest ...Septuagint manuscripts) it The Book of Psalms (from a Greek word indicating songs sung to the accompaniment of stringed instruments). The book was the hymnal of the Jewish people." (Introduction notes from the Ryrie Study Bible)

Psalm 103 starts off with a command, but the command is not God commanding the Psalmist, but the Psalmist commanding his own soul.

SOUL: nephesh (Hebrew) (neh'-fesh)=From H5314; properly a breathing creature, that is, animal or (abstractly) vitality; used very widely in a literal, accommodated or figurative sense (bodily or mental): - any, appetite, beast, body, breath, creature, X dead (-ly), desire, X [dis-] contented, X fish, ghost, + greedy, he, heart (-y), (hath, X jeopardy of) life (X in jeopardy), lust, man, me, mind, mortality, one, own, person, pleasure, (her-, him-, my-, thy-) self, them (your) -selves, + slay, soul, + tablet, they, thing, (X she) will, X would have it. H5314: nâphash (naw-fash')=A primitive root; to breathe; passively, to be breathed upon, that is, (figuratively) refreshed (as if by a current of air): - (be) refresh selves (-ed).

SOUL [Greek] psuchē (psoo-khay')=From G5594; breath, that is, (by implication) spirit, abstractly or concretely (the animal sentient principle only; thus distinguished on the one hand from G4151. G4151: psuchō (psoo'-kho)=A primary verb; to breathe (voluntarily but gently; thus differing on the one hand from G4154, which denotes properly a forcible respiration; and on the other from the base of G109, which refers properly to an inanimate breeze), that is, (by implication of reduction of temperature by evaporation) to chill (figuratively): - wax cold.

The soul is the third part of the trifecta of who we are, what makes up man, wo-man, hu-mans.

> *"Now may the God of Peace Himself sanctify you entirely and may your spirit and soul and body (the trifecta of man) be preserved complete without blame at the coming of our Lord Jesus Christ."*
> ~I Thessalonians 5:23 addition mine

When you boil down the definitions of the soul you come up with the soul being the totality of who we are comprised of; the mind (what we think), the will (volition, free will, choice) and the emotions (the gauge of our feelings).

It is this thing called the soul that the Psalmist (David) is commanding to "bless the Lord." What David is saying "Soul, you bless the Lord." Yes, we can speak to ourselves and order and direct ourselves to do things. Of course this is in conjunction with "all that is within me" to join in the blessings of the Lord.

Our speech flows out of what we believe. If we believe negative, discouraged feelings, misinformation by our friends, teachers, and enemies, when we speak to ourselves it will determine how we act.

> *"And since we have the same spirit of faith, according to what is written, "I believed and therefore I spoke," we also believe and therefore speak, knowing that he which raised up the Lord Jesus shall raise up us also by Jesus, and shall present us with you."*
> ~2 Corinthians 4:13-14, Psalm 116:10

NOTE: The ways it normally works is us requesting the Lord to bless us, even to the point of commanding the Lord to bless us and give us what we want (like benefits). Well, the benefits are already given, and we don't have to request, bet, and cajole the Lord to give them to us. I am not saying that we don't pray/ask the Lord for the blessings, but we don't have to manipulate the Lord to give them to us or to work our way to deserve them; they are already ours.

What we do have to do is remind our souls (ourselves) to "not forget [any] of His benefits," no not one."

NOTE: I find it interesting that the tool for memory is music, a song, a Psalm with stringed instruments. That is why sometimes I will sit down with my guitar and sing songs of remembrance about the goodness of God in the land of the living. (Psalm 27:13)

As we study how to live a maximized, overcoming, more than conqueror, victorious, blessed, prosperous, successful lifestyle, we must remind ourselves of the benefits package, we see that how we speak will determine the actions we take resulting in results.

## THE BENEFITS PACKAGE
- Who pardons all you iniquities.

PARDONS: sâlach (saw-lakh')=A primitive root; to forgive: - forgive, pardon, spare.

ALL: kôl (kole, kole):; properly the whole; hence all, any or every (in the singular only, but often in a plural sense): - (in) all (manner, [ye]), altogether, any (manner), enough, every (one, place, thing), howsoever, as many as, [no-] thing, ought, whatsoever, (the) whole, whoso (-ever).

INIQUITIES: (aw-vone', aw-vone')=From H5753; perversity, that is, (moral) evil: - fault, iniquity, mischief, punishment (of iniquity), sin. H5733: (aw-vaw')=A primitive root; to crook, literally or figuratively: - do amiss, bow down, make crooked, commit iniquity, pervert, (do) perverse (-ly), trouble, X turn, do wickedly, do wrong.

NOTE: We are sinners who are imprisoned by our sins, iniquities, transgressions. The roots of our iniquities stretch back to the Garden as Adam and Eve committed high treason by disobedience (Genesis 2:16-17, Genesis 3:1-19, Romans 5:12). We have a debt that was paid by His amazing grace on the cross.

- Who heals all your diseases

HEALS: râphâ' râphâh (raw-faw', raw-faw')=A primitive root; properly to mend (by stitching), that is, (figuratively) to cure: - cure, (cause to) heal, physician, repair, X thoroughly, make whole.

ALL: kôl kôl (kole, kole)= properly the whole; hence all, any or every (in the singular only, but often in a plural sense): - (in) all (manner, [ye]), altogether, any (manner), enough, every (one, place, thing), howsoever, as many as, [no-] thing, ought, whatsoever, (the) whole, whoso (-ever).

DISEASES: tachălû' tachălû' (takh-al-oo', takh-al-oo')=From H2456; a malady: - disease, X grievous, (that are) sick (-ness). H2456: châlâ, (khaw-law')=A primitive root (compare H2470); to be sick: - be diseased.

NOTE: Sin, sickness, destruction, dis-ease, dis-comfort, dis-stress, dysfunction, anything negative has provision for healing and deliverance. He did not just provide healing for a few, but for *all* dis-eases.
"Surely (no doubt) he has borne our griefs (sicknesses, weaknesses, and distresses) and carried our sorrows and pains [of punishment], yet we [ignorantly] consider him stricken, smitten, and afflicted by god (God did not put on sickness like leprosy) as if with leprosy but (in contrast to) he (Jesus) was wounded for our transgressions (going beyond known limits), he (Jesus) was bruised for our guilt and iniquities (sins); the chastisement [needful to obtain] peace and well-being for us was upon him, and with the stripes (the 39 lashes with a cat of 9 tails=351 stripes) we are healed and made whole). (Isaiah 53:4-5, matthew 8:17 indicated both spiritual and physical healing, the total package like the benefits found in psalm 103:1-5)
NOTE TO THE NOTE: Many people think that sin, sickness, dis-ease, dis-stress, dis-comfort, destruction, and dysfunction is from God, is God's will on earth as it is in heaven. *Wrong.* These people are like those who consider/assume *ignorantly* that God stricken, smitten and afflicted Jesus with dis-ease like leprosy. They are wrong; Jesus came to take away the sin and sickness from our lives on earth (where there is already bad stuff) *as it is* in heaven (where there is forgiveness, healing, ease, destressed, comfort, building up and not tearing down, and function like we are created to be.

- Who redeems your life from the pit

REDEEMS: gâ׳al (gaw-al׳)=A primitive root, to redeem (according to the Oriental law of kinship), that is, to be the next of kin (and as such to buy back a relative's property, marry his widow, etc.): - X in any wise, X at all, avenger, deliver, (do, perform the part of near, next) kinsfolk (-man), purchase, ransom, redeem (-er), revenger.

LIFE: chay (khah'ee)=From H2421; alive; hence raw (flesh); fresh (plant, water, year), strong; also (as noun, especially in the feminine singular and masculine plural) life (or living thing), whether literally or figuratively: - + age, alive, appetite, (wild) beast, company, congregation, life (-time), live (-ly), living (creature, thing), maintenance, + merry, multitude, + (be) old, quick, raw, running, springing, troop. H2421: châyâh (khaw-yaw')= to live, whether literally or figuratively; causatively to revive: - keep (leave, make) alive, X certainly, give (promise) life, (let, suffer to) live, nourish up, preserve (alive), quicken, recover, repair, restore (to life), revive, (X God) save (alive, life, lives), X surely, be whole.

PIT: shachath (shakh'-ath)=From H7743; a pit (especially as a trap); figuratively destruction: - corruption, destruction, ditch, grave, pit. H7743: shûach (shoo'-akh)=A primitive root; to sink, literally or figuratively: - bow down, incline, humble.

   NOTE: Jesus redeemed us from the debt we owed because of Adam and Eve selling out our rights to the d-evil who became the "god of this world who blinds minds" and the "prince of power of air," the father of lies, the accuser of the brethren, the stealer, the killer, the destroyer (II Corinthians 4:4, Ephesians 2:2, John 8:44, Revelation 12:10, John 10:10-29). Jesus save us from the pit, the trap, corruption, destruction and lifted us up.
   4. Who crowns you with lovingkindness and compassion

CROWNS: (aw-tar')=A primitive root; to encircle (for attack or protection); especially to crown (literally or figuratively): - compass, crown.

LOVINGKINDNESS: chêsêd (kheh'-sed)=From H2616; kindness;

by implication (towards God) piety; rarely (by opprobrium) reproof, or (subjectively) beauty: - favour, good deed (-liness, -ness), kindly, (loving-) kindness, merciful (kindness), mercy, pity, reproach, wicked thing. H2616: châsad (khaw-sad')=A primitive root; properly perhaps to bow (the neck only in courtesy to an equal), that is, to be kind; also (by euphemism but rarely) to reprove: - shew self-merciful, put to shame.

COMPASSION/TENDER MERCIES: racham (rakh'-am)=- From H7355; compassion (in the plural); by extension the womb (as cherishing the foetus); by implication a maiden: - bowels, compassion, damsel, tender love, (great, tender) mercy, pity, womb H7355: râcham (raw-kham')=A primitive root; to fondle; by implication to love, especially to compassionate: - have compassion (on, upon), love, (find, have, obtain, shew) mercy (-iful, on, upon), (have) pity, Ruhamah, X surely.

NOTE: Man is called theologically as the "crown of creation" where the Creator created human beings in "Our likeness," in "Our image," and gave them authority/power. The crown in the benefits is twofold: (1) love (2) mercy.

- Who satisfies your years with good things so that your youth is renewed like the eagle.

SATISFIES: (saw-bah', saw-bay'-ah)=A primitive root; to sate, that is, fill to satisfaction (literally or figuratively): - have enough, fill (full, self, with), be (to the) full (of), have plenty of, be satiate, satisfy (with), suffice, be weary of.

GOOD THINGS: (tobe)=From H2895; good (as an adjective) in the widest sense; used likewise as a noun, both in the masculine and the feminine, the singular and the plural (good, a good or good thing, a good man or woman; the good, goods or good things, good men or women), also as an adverb (well): - beautiful, best, better, bountiful, cheerful, at ease, X fair (word), (be in) favour, fine, glad, good (deed,

-lier, liest, -ly, -ness, -s), graciously, joyful, kindly, kindness, liketh (best), loving, merry, X most, pleasant, + pleaseth, pleasure, precious, prosperity, ready, sweet, wealth, welfare, (be) well ([-favoured]).

RENEWED: châdash (khaw-dash')=A primitive root; to be new; causatively to rebuild: - renew, repair.

NOTE: The Rolling Stones sang about not being able to get no satisfaction, but we are promised the benefit of satisfaction, having enough, filled to satisfaction, having enough, having plenty to satiate. We are promised satisfaction with good things and not bad things. We are promised in the benefits to have our strength to be new, rebuilt, and repaired back to a youthful status.

These promises/benefits are accessed by faith in His Word. He said it, we believe it, and that settles. Of course, if He said it that settles it whether we believe it or not. Belief (trusting in, cling to, rely on, adhering to, and cleaving to) His Word by faith opens the door for the principles to work in our life.

## CHAPTER TWENTY-SIX

## THE MINDSET PRINCIPLE

Your mind found in your brain is where you think. How you think is how you speak, and how you speak is how you act.

> *"Unrestrained thoughts (what we think) produces unrestrained words (what we say) resulting in unrestrained actions (what we do).*
> ~From *How to Discipline Your Flesh* by Kenneth Copeland

When Adam and Eve committed high treason in the Garden by disobedience to God's Word, they set into motion death and a curse in the world. The curse is manifested in our thoughts, our words, and our actions which impacts our lifestyle and hinders us from living a maximized, overcoming, more than conqueror, victorious, blessed, prosperous, successful lifestyle and causes us to live a minimized, being overcome, less than conqueror, losing, cursed, poverty, failure lifestyle. Yes, God is the answer to all of our problems, but we have been given the authority to take control of our lives, with the help of the anointing of God and the Holy Spirit.

> *"For those who are (walking) according (based on) to the flesh set their minds (mindset) on the things of the flesh (carnal nature), but those who are (walking) according to the Spirit, (Holy) the things of the (Holy) Spirit."*
> ~Romans 8:5 addition mine

> *"The mind set (our mindset) on the flesh (carnal nature) is death*

but *(in contrast) the mind set (mindset) on the Spirit (the Holy Spirit) is life and peace."*

~Romans 8:6 addition mine

Zig Ziglar called wrong thinking (mindset) "stinking thinking."

James Allen's book *As a Man Thinketh* states that "we are what we think".

Napoleon Hill declared, "Whatever the mind of man can conceive and believe, it can achieve," and "The starting point of all achievement is desire."

Norman Vincent Peale, to many the guru for positive thinking states, "Our happiness depends on the habit of mind we cultivate. So practice happy thinking every day."

> *"Thought in the mind hath made us. What we are by thought was wrought and builit. If a man's mind hath evil thoughts, pain comes on him as comes the wheel the ox behind...if one endure the purity of thought, joy follows him as his own shadow sure."*
>
> ~The Buddha

Some may be upset by me quoting positive thinkers and even The Buddha, but Paul cites a pagan poet to condemn his theological foe, who apparently came from the Island of Crete. He says,

> *"As one of them, a prophet of their own once said, 'Cretans have always been liars vicious beasts and lazy gluttons.'"*
>
> ~Titus 1:12

We love to quote the Golden Rule found in Leviticus 19:18 and quoted by Jesus in Matthew 17:12/Luke 6:31, "Do unto others as you would have them do unto you." Confucius is also credited with the words of wisdom. Confucius himself made the Golden Rule an unrivaled centerpiece of his philosophy of life (The Analects, 1962). The thread of the Golden Rule flows in many religions, but Jesus quoted it from Leviticus 17:12 and owned it.

I have mentioned before that many positive thinkers have taken

Biblical concepts and put them out as principles of a P.M.A., a positive mental attitude. That does not make them bad or wrong, but it falls short of realizing maximum potential. Maximum potential is unlocked by faith towards God and not faith towards self. Man can take all the Biblical principles and all the human beliefs, but will still fall short and end up with the religion of Humanism; the worship of themselves. When our faith is towards God (Hebrews 6:1) and His power is towards us (Ephesians 1:19), the point of contact is where God's *super* comes on our *natural*.

The Bible states, "For as he thinketh in his heart, so is he: Eat and drink, saith he to thee; but his heart is not with thee." (Pro-Verbs 23:7, King James Versions with all the thee, thou and saiths).

The Mindset Principle will change the course and trajectory of your life. It does not matter what profession or circumstance that you find yourself in, what you think will produce words you say and affect how you act. Man, wo-man, and hu-mans are three part beings that were affected by the fall in the Garden as a result of A & E's (Adam and Eve) high treason via disobedience to God's commands (Genesis 2:16-17, Genesis 3:1-19) Jesus hung on the cross and became a curse in our place (Galatians 3:10-14). Our human spirit, the lamp of the Lord. (Pro-Verbs 20:27)

A lamp (not a candle) in the Bible days was a made of clay, filled with oil, and then the wick was lit. It was a source of light in darkness making the home intimate, giving comfort, illuminating. When the wick was snuffed out, darkness. I am convinced that the lamp of the Lord, the human spirit when filled with oil (the Holy Spirit) and the wick lit, gave out light, intimacy, illumination—where the fruit grows, the Spirit flows. In the Garden at the point of disobedience, the wick was snuffed out, and there was a need for the lamp to be relit. I believe that the flint of the cross and Jesus relit the lamp when people believed (trusted in, clung to, relied on, adhered to) the D.B.R. (Death, Burial, Resurrection) of Jesus. I believe this is what needed saving, the spirit, little s, the human spirit.

The soul (the mind, what we think), (the will, what we choose) and the emotions (the gauge of our feelings) are not what was saved, like the spirit. The mind must be renewed, a new mindset must be developed, and this is progressive while the emotions follow suit. Where your mind goes so goes the emotions.

The body (flesh, blood, bones, nervous systems, the skeletal system, and the organs of the body) is still subject to the curse on earth. So when you accept Jesus as your savior, and you are saved, born again, it is the spirit. If you died one second after you said yes to Jesus, you are in heaven, absent from the body and present with the Lord. (2 Corinthians 5:8)

I preached a funeral for my mother-in-law who died of cancer in her physical body. During the funeral, I motioned to the casket holding her body, and mentioned how the body was like a peanut shell. She had died, but the body remained, and then I said that the shell was still here but the *nut* was gone. Waves of laughter went through the funeral home. The funeral director came and told me that was the best funeral he had ever attended.

When we get saved, we are new creations in Christ, but we are still housed in physical bodies that are still corrupting. Eventually, we will get a new body, but until then we have to exercise, we have to eat right. The same with the soul. Yes, we are saved, but like the body we still have to work on our mind, our will, and our emotions. Left to our own devices, the mind will soak in whatever we watch, whatever we hear, and whatever we speak to ourselves. Like we saw in the previous chapter about *The Benefits Package*, the Psalmist spoke to his soul and told the soul what to do, which was to bless the Lord and to remember all of the benefits (Psalm 103:1-5)

Like we exercise the body we must exercise the mind, and the way that we exercise the mind is by renewing the mind.

*"Above all else, guard your heart, for everything you do flows from it."*
~Pro-Verbs 4:23

NOTE: You heart is the core of your being; some call it the innermost man. There is a deep link between the human spirit and the mind, so when you guard your heart, you guard your mind. Everything in your life from your work to your worship flows out of your spirit-mind. Philippians 4:6 states,

*"Be anxious (in your mind) for nothing but in everything by prayer, supplication with thanksgiving let your request be made known to God. And the peace of God (in your mind filled with anxiety) will guard your hearts and your minds (the battlefield) in Christ Jesus.*

I believe that by renewing your mind with the Word of God, you have set the guard around what you think.

*"And do not be conformed to this world, but be transformed by the renewing of your mind, so that you may prove what the will of God is, that which is good and acceptable and perfect."*
~Romans 12:2

NOTE: We are called to be transformed (like the metamorphosis of a butterfly) and to not be conformed (shaped into a mold) to this world (the thinking of this world). This transformation comes by the renewing (making new versus staying old) of your mind. The cause and effect is the proving, the evidence of what the will of God is. The will of God is (1) good (2) acceptable (3) perfect unlike the will of the d-evil which is (1) bad (2) unacceptable (3) imperfect. When you pray with a renewed mind you will pray the good, acceptable perfect will of God on earth as it is in heaven.

*"Therefore, if you have been raised up with Christ, keep seeking the things above, where Christ is seated at the right hand of God. Set your minds on things above, not on earthly things (things that are on the earth."*
~Colossians 3:1-2

NOTE: When you set your mind, you are making a choice to focus your mind on something that is not here on earth. You are looking towards heavenly things. This makes sense to me that as you are praying for the good, perfect, and acceptable will of God on earth as it is in heaven that you look to heaven. *If* you can find sickness, poverty, negative and bad things then pray that to come to earth, *but* we already have those things on earth so we don't need to pray those things or accept those things that are sent by the d-evil on earth as it is in hell.

> *"The mind governed (set) by the flesh is death, but the mind governed (set) by the Spirit is life and peace."*
> ~Romans 8:6 addition mine

NOTE: How we think is how things will happen to us here on earth, flesh/death/negative things happens hinged on your mindset (what you think) and you mouthset (what you speak) while Spirit/life/peace/positive things happens hinged on your mindset (what you think and your mouthset (what you speak). We will look at the mindset later in this chapter.

> *"Finally, brothers and sisters, whatever is true, whatever is noble, whatever is right, whatever is pure, whatever is lovely, whatever is admirable–if anything is excellent or praiseworthy–think about such things (let/allow your mind to dwell on these things."*
> ~Philippians 4:8

NOTE: This verse is in connection with anxiety in your mind versus peace guarding your hearts and your minds in Christ Jesus. The old saying is, "where you are dwelling, will be telling." The word "let" indicates that we have a choice of what we let our minds dwell on.

> *"But you did not learn Christ in this way, if indeed you have heard Him and have been taught in Him, just as truth is in Jesus, that, in reference to your former manner of life, you lay aside the old self, which is being corrupted in accordance with the lusts of deceit, and that you be renewed in the spirit of your mind, and put on the new self, which in the likeness of God has been created in righteousness and holiness of the truth."*
> ~Ephesians 4:20-24

NOTE: When you became a Christian you became a new creation. The old creation was filled with empty words, immorality, sensuality, impurity, corruption. This old mind is to be renewed in the spirit of your mind. You are then responsible to put on the new self. We take off the old self (like an old coat) and falsehoods, and speak truth. We are called to "let no unwholesome word proceed from your mouth…" but let wholesome words good for edification to proceed from your mouth. A renewed mind, will produce wholesome edifying words. (Ephesians 4:20-32)

The words that you speak come out of your belief system and also out of your unbelief system. You choose the systems by how you set your mind.

We are called to;

> "…not walk according to the flesh but (walk) according to the Spirit."
>
> Romans 8:4 addition mine

NOTE: Some Christians are looking for their calling like it is some elusive thing that God is keeping secret from them. We are called to walk in His steps that He set by example. (I Peter 2:21) The walk includes what you say with your mouth which is a reflection of your mindset.

> "For those who are (walking) according to the flesh, set the minds (mindset) on the things of the flesh (carnal nature), but (in contrast to) those who are (walking) according to the Spirit (The Holy Spirit) (set their minds on) the things of the Spirit (The Holy Spirit)."
>
> ~Romans 8:5 addition mine.

NOTE: The walk is a pattern that you are following. Straight is the gate and narrow the way, but sometimes you meet a fork in the road as they diverge. One road is the flesh, and the other road is the Spirit. If your mind is renewed then it will act like a GPS and lead you down the right road. It is all hinged on your mindset.

> "For the mind set (mindset) on the flesh (carnal nature) is death

*(separation from God) BUT (in contrast to) the mind set (mindset) on the Spirit (Holy Spirit) is life (abundant) and peace (wholeness and rest)."*

~Romans 5:6 addition mine

NOTE: A mindset, the setting of your mind, is a choice.

*"I call heaven and earth to witness against you today, that I have set before you life and death, the blessing and the curse. So choose life in order that you may live, you and your descendants."*

~Deuteronomy 30:19

Choose wisely my friends.

*"Because the mind set (mindset) is hostile toward God; for it (the mind) does not subject itself (yield) to the law of God, for it is not even able to do so (it may try but it can't)."*

~Romans 8:7 addition mine

NOTE: Have you ever been in a relationship that is hostile? You fight, you bicker, you're hurt each other by your words, you sulk and pout, and you are miserable. That describes the relationship between you and God. He just take it in and loves you but you are guilty and ashamed. When you renew you mind, you begin to think differently and yield your will towards Him and the hostility melts away.

*"For those who are in the flesh (the carnal nature) cannot please God."*

~Romans 8:8 addition mine

NOTE: We were created to be God-lovers and the way that we love God can only be accomplished by faith in Him and in His word. We see in Hebrews11:6 that, "without faith it is impossible to please Him, for he who comes to God must believe that His is (that He exists) and that He is a rewarder of those who (diligently) seek Him (and not just passively inquire). (Hebrews 11:6) When we hear his

Word, faith comes. When we renew our minds, faith keeps coming and our desire is not to be hostile towards Him but to please Him.

> *"However you are* not *in the flesh* but *(you are)* in *the Spirit,* if indeed the Spirt of God dwells in you. but *if anyone does not have the Spirit of Christ (in him), he does not belong to Him.* if *Christ is in you though the body is dead because of sin yet the spirit (human spirit, the lamp of the Lord) because of righteousness. But if the Spirit of Him (the Holy Spirit) who raised Christ Jesus from the dead will also give life to your mortal bodies through His Spirit (Holy Spirit) who* dwells in you *(in your human spirit, little s, the lamp of the Lord)."*
> ~Romans 8:9-11 addition mine

If you want to live a maximized, overcoming, more than conqueror, victorious, blessed, prosperous and successful lifestyle, then you need to develop your mindset.

## CHAPTER TWENTY-SEVEN

## THE COFFEE CUP THEOLOGY PRINCIPLE

This is one of my favorite principles. As you live and walk out your life in this cursed and fallen world, you have the opportunity to be like an Elvis Presley song. You can become all shook up.

For many years (around 27 years) in the Ruminator Sunday School Class, I would use an example about what comes out of our mouths. The principle relates to our last chapter about our minds—that are either renewed or not renewed—what is in our minds spews out of our mouths all over us and others near to us.

I would scope out the people in the class and find someone who was new and had not heard my coffee cup theology principle. If they had a cup of coffee, I would ask them to move their Bible and papers. The rest of the class that knew what was coming began to giggle as the newbie began to get nervous. I would then ask them to gently shake their cup. The coffee in the cup began to slosh around but not enough to come out of the cup. I would then ask them to shake it harder and harder and harder and then suddenly, coffee came out of the cup everywhere on the table. Of course they had shocked looks, and the class was laughing.

I then asked, "Why did coffee come out of your cup?" The standard response was, "Because you made me shake the cup." No, the reason *coffee* came out of the cup is because that's what was in the cup. The shaking only revealed what was in the cup.

The world is full things that shake us up; everything from politics, elections, Wall Street with fluctuating numbers, physicians with bad diagnoses and prognoses, Facebook, unreasonable friends, work, bosses (your fill in the blank with whatever pushes your buttons).

What comes out of your mouth, what you internalize, what feelings are harder are expressed, because that is what in you. The external pressures only reveal what is in your heart (your cup). The same principle applies with something other than coffee.

In our analogy, the cup is our heart. The heart is not to be left alone unguarded, because if it is left unguarded anything can sneak in and fill it.

> *"Watch over (guard) your heart (cup) with all diligence, for from it (the heart/cup) flow the springs of life."*
> ~Pro-Verbs 4:23 addition mine

NOTE: The shaking of the cup/heart reveals what is in the cup—coffee, or hot chocolate. We chose what fills our heart by what we renew our minds on.

> *"As a man thinketh so is he."*
> ~Pro-Verbs 23:7

I imagine a funnel coming down from the brain (the thinker) into the heart (spirit, cup). When shaken what you are thinking will come out the mouth.

> *"The good man out of the good treasure of his heart brings forth what is good; and the evil man out of the evil treasure brings forth what is evil; for his mouth speaks from that which fills his heart."*
> ~Luke 6:45

NOTE: Many positive thinkers think that *being good* and *speaking good things* is the *key to success*. While these Biblical principles may work to a point, the full effect of Biblical principles working to their full potential is hinged on being good/righteous. The problem is that without Jesus, "there is none righteous/good, no not one." (Romans 3:10, Psalm 14:1-3). Being good is not enough, for "all have sinned and fall short of the glory of God." (Romans 6:23)

*"The bad man/sinner out of the bad treasure of his heart brings forth what is bad; and the evil/bad man out of the evil/bad treasure brings for what is evil/bad; for his mouth speaks from that which fills his heart (bad things).*

~Romans 6:23 addition mine

*"Set a guard, O Lord, over my mouth; keep watch over the door of my lips, do not incline my heart to any evil thing, to practice deeds of wickedness with men who do iniquity, and do not let me eat their delicacies."*

~Psalm 141:10

NOTE: The Psalmist realizes the mouth is the exit port of the heart. He is asking for help from God and wants a guard set over his mouth. He wants God's help to keep watch of the door (exit port) of his lips. He realizes that the heart is inclined to evil. Many people say when they are making decision for their lives, "I'm just following my heart." That's the problem.

*"The heart (the cup) is more deceitful than all else and is desperately sick; who can understand it?"*

~Jeremiah 17:9 addition mine

Is it any wonder that when the deceitful and desperately sick heart/cup is shaken that what comes out of the cup is deceitful and desperately sick words?

*"Now on the last day, the great day of the feast, Jesus stood and cried out, saying, if anyone is thirsty, let him come to Me and drink. He who believes (trusts in, clings to, relies on, adheres to, cleaves to) Me (Jesus), as the Scriptures said (Isaiah 44:3, Isaiah 55:1, Isaiah 58:11) from his innermost being will flow rivers of living water. But this He spoke of the Spirit (Holy), whom those who believed (trusted in, clung to, relied on, adhered to, cleaved to) in Him (Jesus) were to receive; for the Spirit (Holy) was not yet given, because Jesus was not yet glorified (D.B.R. plus returned to the Father)."*

~John 7:37 addition mine

NOTE: The feast (one of three festivals) that is called the Feast of Booths occurs in the autumn after harvest. The tradition of this festival was that they would build booths from the boughs of trees and dwell in them for the seven days of the festival (Ryrie Study Bible notes on John 7:2) On the last day (some say it was the seventh day, and some say the eight day) of the great feast Jesus stood up and made a pronouncement.

"Though it is not mentioned in the O.T., the Jews had a ceremony of carrying water from the Pool of Siloam and pouring it into the silver basin by the altar of burnt offering. Each day. On the eight day this was not done, making Christ's offer of water of eternal life from Himself even more startling." (Ryrie Study Bible note on John 7:37-39)

When you drink from Jesus (the Word who was in the beginning with God and who *was* God, John 1:1-14) something happens. From out of the person who drinks the water there will be a flow rivers (not just a trickle) of living (alive) waters. Jesus then clarifies whom He was talking about, The Spirit (Holy) of God. The innermost being is the belly/core/spirit/cup that was filled with the Holy Spirit of God.

> *"If you have been foolish in exalting yourself or if you have plotted evil, put your hand over your mouth. For the churning of milk produces butter, and pressing the nose brings forth blood; so the churning of anger produces strife."*
> ~Pro-Verbs 30:32

NOTE: Once again we see that prideful, evil plotting is stopped at the mouth. The example of plotting evil is a butter churn, and the churning is the agitation that produces what is in the churn. The churning, the agitation of milk, produces butter, and the pressing/pinching of the nose brings forth blood. There is cause and effect of what we do. The same is true for the churning of anger; it produces strife. In this case we see the churn is the heart, the cup, and what is in the churn/heart/cup is being agitated/stirred up. What is in the churn is what overflows out of the mouth. Again, shake the cup, coffee comes out of the cup because that is what was in the cup—the shaking, the agitation merely reveals what is in the cup. However, if you put cream, sugar, peaches (or any other delicious fruit or candy) the churning of the ingredients produces delicious ice cream. The same churn, the same heart, the same cup, but different ingredients producing different results. What's in your churn?

> *"How can a young man (or wo-man) keep his/her way pure? By keeping it according to your Word. With all my heart I have sought You; do not let me wander from Your commandments. Your Word I have hid (treasured) in my heart (cup) that I may not sin against You."*
> ~Psalm 119:9-11 addition mine

NOTE: Sin is the downfall of the believer. Sin is usually manifested in our words. We can usually cover up our sins from people, and we can talk differently around others, but when the pressure is on your heart and mind will be revealed with your words and actions. However we can deal with our impure thoughts and words by keeping it (our way) according to (based on) the Word of God. We must seek Him with all of our heart. We hid the Word, treasure the word in our heart/cup. When we do that we will not sin/speak against the Lord.

# CHAPTER TWENTY-EIGHT

## THE MOUNTAIN MOVING PRINCIPLE

This principle can really be a combination of the prayer principle and the faith principle. Prayer is merely a conversation with the Creator of the universe. Without faith it is impossible to please Him and if we want to please Him (Hebrews 11:6) in our prayer life, we must:
- Come to Him
- Believe that He is (exists)
- Believe that He is a rewarder of those who diligently seek Him and not just passively inquire of Him.

To have a maximized, overcoming, more than conqueror, victorious, blessed, prosperous and good success lifestyle, it will have to be by faith as you face the mountains in your life.

You know, those mountains that stand between you and what you want and need, as the mountain looms over you creating the shadow that casts doom and gloom over you. So, where does faith fit into the equation of dealing with the mountains in your life? It all hinges on five words.

1. Have
2. Faith
3. In
4. God
5. Constantly

### THE KEY TO MOUNTAIN MOVING FAITH

Jesus, who came to earth via a virgin birth (aka Christmas) grew up for 30 years (no one knows exactly what he was doing) and then he was baptized (dipped) by John the Dipper (Baptist).

NOTE: John was not a Baptist but part of a sect of Jews called the Essenes, and should be called John the Essene.

Jesus was baptized by John in the Jordan River (Matthew 3:1-15) and when He came up out of the water the Holy Spirit came upon Him in the form of a dove. (John 3:16-17) After that He was led by the Holy Spirit through the wilderness and was tempted by the d-evil for 40 days for the purpose of drawing Jesus away from His purpose and destiny. Jesus' purpose was to "destroy the works of the d-evil." (I John 3:8) For three years Jesus developed his Modus Operandi (M.O.) (Matthew 4:23-24)

> *"Jesus was going throughout all Galilee (1) teaching in their synagogues (2) and proclaiming the Gospel (good news) of the Kingdom (3) and healing every kind of sickness and every kind of disease among the people.*
> ~Matthew 4:23 addition mine

The will of God on earth as it was in heaven was manifested by Jesus as He healed:
- every kind of sickness
- every kind of disease
- all who were ill
- suffering
- various kinds of dis-ease
- pains
- demoniacs
- epileptics
- paralytics.

Jesus handled these various mountains as He healed them.

Jesus expected people to have faith, but this faith was not in other people, things, situations, circumstances but in God. The Amplified Bible states it this way:

> *"Have faith in God, constantly."*

Our faith should be in God 7/24/365. To me this like pray

without ceasing. Whenever anything comes up I turn to God in prayer by faith.

Jesus had passed through Jerusalem and saw some things that He did not like, but He kept on going until He reached Bethany. Jesus and the boys most likely rested, had supper, and then went to bed. The next morning Jesus woke up and was preparing to return to Jerusalem and the temple to clean house, using a cat of nine tails as His broom. Jesus saw a fig tree from the distance and wondered if perhaps there were some figs on the leafy tree, but the time of figs had passed, and no figs were to be found. So Jesus cursed the tree.

> *"He (Jesus) said to it (the fig tree), May no one ever eat fruit from you again."*
> ~Mark 11:14 addition mine

What an odd thing to do, speak to an inanimate object. He then headed out back to Jerusalem and proceeded to drive out those who were buying and selling in the temple, and overturned the tables of the money changers and the seats of those who were selling doves; and He would not permit anyone to carry merchandise through the temple. Then He began to teach. Modern day preachers like to start off with a joke, but it appears that Jesus like to warm up the crowd with a little one man riot. (See Mark 11:12-19) After returning to Bethany, Jesus and the boys passed the fig tree that He had spoken to, and they saw (with their eyes) the fig tree withered from the roots up.

Peter remembered what had happened that morning when they left, and he said to Jesus, "Rabbi, look, the fig tree which you cursed (by speaking words) has withered." This is where it gets good. Jesus did not act surprised as if something unusual had happened. No, He merely related it to faith.

> *"And Jesus answered saying to them, 'have faith in God, constantly.'"*
> ~Mark 11:22 (AMP)

Jesus took this moment and made it a teachable moment about how to pray a prayer with constant faith in God.

MARK 11:23
1. Whoever says to this mountain (1) Be taken up (2) Be cast into the sea
2. Does not doubt in his heart
3. But believes (trusts in, clings to, relies on, adheres to and cleaves to) what he says (to the mountain) is going to happen
4. It (what he says to the mountain) will be (in the future) granted him.

MARK 11:24
1. Therefore (in reference to what He had just said in Mark 11:23)
2. All things (not just mountains) for which you pray (a conversation with God and/or speaking to a mountain), ask (specifically), believe (not doubt but trusting in, clinging to, relying on, adhering to and cleaving to)
3. You have (not going to but have them now) received them (the prayers)
4. They (the prayers) will be granted you (answered).

MARK 11:25
1. Whenever you stand praying (in the standing posture of prayer and digging in your heels taking a stand in prayer)
2. Forgive: (a) Let it drop (b) Leave it (c) Let it go
3. Forgive Triple AAA Style (a) Anything (a) Against (a) Anyone
4. In order that your Father Who is in heaven may also forgive you your own failings and shortcomings
5. Let them drop

MARK 11:26
1. If you do not forgive
2. Neither will your Father in heaven
3. Forgive your failings and shortcomings.

NOTE: Some verses do not contain verse 26.

## PRACTICAL APPLICATION

I suggest taking a piece of paper and drawing a mountain range. Then write the name of whatever your specific mountain is. It could be arthritis, depression, poverty etc. Then write the name of Jesus above the mountain range. Jesus' name is the name named that is above all names (Philippians 2:9-11) Then as you exercise your faith continually, speak out loud to the named mountains and tell the mountains exactly what you want to happen.

If you are going to live a maximized, overcoming, more than conqueror, victorious, blessed, prosperous and successful lifestyle, you will b living by faith and not by sight, you will speak forth faith, you will pray and believe and not doubt, and you will forgive anything, against, anyone.

# CHAPTER TWENTY-NINE

## THE GOOD REPORT PRINCIPLE
## AKA THE GRASSHOPPER PRINCIPLE

In this chapter we see a principle that helps us to look at ourselves, and if we see what we don't like then we can change it. These various principles are found in Numbers 13: 1-33.

The children of Israel had been set free from the bondage of the taskmasters and the Pharaoh. They had a promise of the Promised Land, a land that flowed with milk and honey. They had been wandering in the wilderness for 40 years in what should have been an eleven-day journey.

> "It is eleven days' journey from Horeb by the way of Mount Seir to Kadesh-barnea."
>
> ~Deuteronomy 1:11

> "The LORD our God spoke to us at Horeb, saying, 'You have stayed long enough at this mountain.'"
>
> ~Deuteronomy 1:6

There was a Promised Land for them to go in and possess the land.

> "See, I have placed the land before you; go in and possess the land which the LORD swore to give to your fathers, to Abraham, to Isaac, and to Jacob, to them and their descendants after them."
>
> ~Deuteronomy 1:9

As they were on the other side of Canaan (the land flowing with milk and honey), the Lord spoke to Moses to set up a reconnaissance mission to cross over and spy out the land. (Numbers 13:2) The ones selected for the mission were the elite of the tribes who were the "heads of the sons of Israel." (Numbers 13:3-16) There were two who were responsible for bringing back a good report versus a bad and evil report (1) Caleb from the tribe of Judah (praise) the son of Jephunneh (b) Hoshea the son of Nun, Joshua from the tribe of Ephraim. (Numbers 13:6,8). Eleven were sent to spy out the land but Joshua, the son of Nun was called. (Numbers 13:16)

NOTE: God was not sending them out to spy the land to see what the conditions were but to let them see that what He had said was true. The orders for the mission is found in Numbers 13:17-20.

1. Go up there in to the Negev and then go up into the hill country.
2. See what the land is like
3. See whether the people who live in it are strong or weak
4. See whether the people who live in it are few of many
5. How is the land in which they live?
6. Is the land good or bad?
7. How are the cities in which they live?
8. Are the cities like open camps or with fortification?
9. How is the land?
10. Is the land fat or lean?
11. Are there trees in it or not?
12. Make an effort to get some of the fruit of the land

There were 12 men and 12 orders.

> *"So they went up and spied ou the land from the wilderness of Zin as far as Rehob, at Lebo-hamath. They saw that there were (1) inhabitants in the land (2) Some were giants (the descendants of Anak).*
>
> ~Numbers 13:21-22 addition mine

They entered into the valley of Eschol and they cut down a branch with a single cluster of grapes, and they carried this single cluster of grapes on a pole between two men, with some of the pomegranates and the figs. (Numbers 13:23) Now that must have been some big grapes. I can only imagine how big the pomegranates and the figs were. This place was called the valley of Eschol, because of the cluster which the sons of Israel cut down from there.

## RETURN FROM THE MISSION WITH A REPORT SHOW AND TELL TIME

The twelve spies returned from their mission at the end of 40 days. They came to Moses and Aaron and to All the congregation of the sons of Israel in the wilderness of Paran at Kadesh; and they brought back word to them and to all the congregation and showed them the fruit. (Numbers 13:25-26) Thus they told him (Moses), (1) We went in to the land where you sent us (2) It certainly does flow with milk and honey and this is the fruit. (Numbers 13:27)
NEVERTHELESS & MOREOVER
1. The people who live in the land are strong
2. The cities are fortified and very large
3. We saw the descendants of Anak
4. Amalek is living in the land
5. Living in the hill country (a) Hittites, Jebusites Amorites
6. Living by the sea and by the side of Jordan are the Canaanites

At this point the people began loudly grumbling and complaining.

Then Caleb quieted the people before Moses and said, "We should *by all means* go up and take possession of it (the land), for *we shall overcome it*. Now that is what a good report sounds like. That is what walking, living, speaking by faith looks like. If you are going to live a maximized, overcoming, more than conqueror, victorious, successful, and prosperous lifestyle, this is how you must think, speak, and act.

Once Caleb spoke forth victory, he had to quiet the people down. Remember the people had to be quieted down in front of Moses. The elite warriors who had gone up with Joshua and Caleb threw in their two cents.

"But the men who had gone up with him (Caleb) said, We are *not able* to go up against the people, for they are *too strong for us*."

## GOOD REPORT BAD REPORT

Good report: We should by all means go up and take possession of it for we shall surely overcome it. (Numbers 13:30)

Bad report: We are not able to go up against the people for they are too strong for us.

It does not matter if you work in a corporation or a small mom and pop shop, if you are a minister or *just* a Christian, you will be faced with making choices (1) Bad choices (2) Good choices. You will be faced with (1) Good reports (2) Bad reports. While faith comes by hearing the Word of God, so does doubt and unbelief comes by hearing the words the d-evil and negative people. It all hinges on whose report you are going to believe. If you are wise, you will believe the report of the Lord!

## HOW YOU SEE YOURSELF IS HOW THE ENEMY SEES YOU

The bad report included;

> *"The land through which we have gone, in spying it out is a land that devours its inhabitants and all the people whom we saw in it are men of great size."*
>
> ~Numbers 13:32

### NOTE:

This was reality. It was not a false report, it was just a bad report.

> *"There also we saw the Nephilim (the sons of Anak who were part of the Nephilim, giants); and we* became *(went from warriors to fearful men) like grasshoppers* in our own sight, *and so we* were in their sight.*"*

If you can catch hold of this principle you will change the mindset of who you are *in Christ* (in the anointing of God).

## CHAPTER THIRTY

# THE COMMUNICATION SYSTEM PRINCIPLE

In the beginning God created the heavens and the earth. God took chaos and brought order to it. (Genesis 1:1-1-25) Then God created man (male and female) in "Our image" and in "Our likeness"

> *"Then God said, let Us make man in Our image, according to Our likeness…"*
>
> ~Genesis 1:26

NOTE: I believe that the "Our" is plural and includes (1) The Father (2) The Son (3) The Holy Ghost.

> *"God created man in His own image; in the image of God He created him; male and female He created them."*
>
> ~Genesis 1:27

When God first created a man (Genesis 2:6) and man became a living being, God began communicating with him.

> *"The Lord God commanded the man saying from any tree of the garden you may eat freely, but from the tree of the knowledge of good and evil you shall not eat, for in the day that you eat from it, you shall surely die."*
>
> ~Genesis 2:16-17

Then God created the woman and instituted the marriage between a man and a woman. (Genesis 2:21-25) There would be communication between the husband and wife and between Creator and creation. After the fall of disobedience when Adam and Eve committee high treason, there was a disruption in the free, clear communication system between them and God. The frequency was jammed by sin, iniquity, transgression. Communication was restored at the cross with the D.B.R., Death, Burial, and Resurrection of Jesus.

Prayer is the link to heaven, The Word of God is the Codebook and Faith is the wave-length connection between God and you.

> *"For the word of the cross (The Broadcast Tower) is foolishness to those who ae perishing, but to us who are being saved (having communication reestablished) it is the power (duNAMis, dynamic, miraculous, dynamic ability, to communicate with God)."*
> ~I Corinthians 1:18 addition mine

NOTE: Words are what we use to communicate to one another. We speak (pray) and He responds back (with the Word) thus co-mmunication and not just a one-way conversation. When He speaks, it lines up with His Code Book (The Word of God.

While the communication was disrupted at the fall in the Garden over the tree, communication was reestablished at a tree outside of the Garden in Jerusalem called the Garden of Gethsemane on a hill called Calvary. The lost link was restored as our spirit, the lamp of the Lord was restored. I believe that the human spirit is where communication with the Lord is established. Within the human spirit is the Holy Spirit, the divine link between us and God. In the human spirit, there is revelation, intimacy with the Lord (like they had in the Garden before the fall), a place where the fruit can grow and the gifts can flow. In other places in this book we talked about revealed mysteries. The place of revelation is with the spirit (little s) by the Big S (the Holy Spirit).

> *"But just as it is written (Isaiah 64:4, Isaiah 65:17), Things which eye has not seen and ear has not entered the heart of man all that God has prepared for those who love Him."*
> ~I Corinthians 2:9 addition mine

*"The secret things belong to the Lord our God, but the things revealed belong to us and to our sons forever, that we may observe all he words of this law."*
~Deuteronomy 29:29

The spirit (little s) connection with the Spirit (big S) is where our communication system was established.

*"In the same way (groaning within, Romans 8:23-25) the Spirit (big S) also helps our weakness; for we do not know how to pray (communicate with God) as we should, but the Spirit (big S) Himself intercedes for us with groaning's/utterances too deep for words and He who searches the hearts knows what the mind of the Spirit is, because He intercedes for the saints according to the will of God."*
~Romans 8:26-27 addition mine

NOTE: We have communication between God/Jesus/The Holy Spirit via the communication system.

*"For to us God revealed (communicated) them (things not seen, heard, and not entered the heart of man) through the Spirit; for the Spirit searches all things, even the depths (heart) of God. For who among men know the thoughts of man except the spirit (little s) of the man which is in him (the exact location of the spirit of man)? Even so the thoughts of God no one knows except the Spirit (Big S) of God (Who dwells in our spirit, little s, the lamp of the Lord)."*
~I Corinthians 2:10-11 addition mine

NOTE: Spirit to spirit communication takes place as we believe in the Death, Burial and Resurrection of Jesus.

*"Now we (believers) have received not the spirit of the world (the spirit of Antichrist), but (we have received) the Spirit Who is from God, so that we may know the things feely given to us by God, which things we also speak not, in words taught by human wisdom,*

*but in those taught by the Spirit, combining spiritual thought with spiritual words."*

~I Corinthians 2:12-13 addition mine

NOTE: The spirit of the world disrupts the frequency between us and God. Spiritual thoughts (a renewed mind, renewed by the Word of God (spiritual words) is found in the Codebook of Communication (The Word of God)

*"But having the same spirit of faith, according to what is written, "I believed, therefore I spoke," we also believe, therefore we also speak, knowing that He who raised the Lord Jesus will raise us also with Jesus and will present us with you."*

~2 Corinthians 4:13-14

## CHAPTER THIRTY-ONE

## THE LOVE PRINCIPLE

I saved this chapter for the last. In my mind all of the principles are good principles, but if they are not motivated out of love, this is just another book about positive thinking.

Jackie Deshannon once admonished us that the world needs love, sweet love, and needs it now.

The Beatles added that the only thing we need is love, love, love. But Larry Norman observed that after making that declaration, they broke up.

LOVE (noun) (1) a profoundly tender, passionate affection for another person. (2) A feeling of warm personal attachment or deep affection, as for a parent, child, or friend. (3) Sexual passion or desire.

LOVE: (verb) (1) To have love or affection for: (2) to have a profoundly tender, passionate affection for (another person). (2) To have a strong liking for; take great pleasure (3) To need or require; benefit greatly from (4) To embrace and kiss (someone), to have sexual intercourse with (5) To have love or affection for another person; be in love.

> *"For God so loved (agape') the world that He gave His only begotten Son (Jesus) that whosoever believed (trusted in, clung to, relied on, adhered to, cleaved to) in Him (Jesus) should not perish but have everlasting life."*
>
> ~John 3:16 addition mine

> *"The one who does not love does not know God, for God is love."*
> ~I John 4:8

> *"We love, because He first loved us."*
> ~I John 4:19

This thing called love is not a man-made emotion but a God influenced emotion. God initiated it, mankind received it, and we were created to give this God-Love to other human beings. In the Garden when the fall took place as Adam and Eve committed high treason through disobedience, love was perverted and became lust.

LUST: epithumia (ep-ee-thoo-mee'-ah)=From G1937; a longing (especially for what is forbidden): - concupiscence (sexual desire; lust, ardent, usually sensuous, longing, desire, lust (after).G1937: epithumeō (ep-ee-thoo-meh'-oto set the heart upon, that is, long for (rightfully or otherwise): - covet, desire, would fain, lust (after).

Lust included lasciviousness, licentiousness which means to be unrestrained. True love restrains lust.

> *"Without a vision, the people perish."*
> ~Pro-Verb 29:18

> *"Without a vision the people are unrestrained."*
> ~Pro-Verbs 29:18

> *"Without a fresh prophetic revelatory Word from Jehovah my people will be and even now are perishing and being annihilated"*
> ~Pro-Verbs 29:18 (Kirk DeVinney personal translation

Lust kills, God love heals. We must restrain lust.

> *"Unrestrained thoughts (what we think) produces unrestrained words (what we say) resulting in unrestrained actions (what we do)."*
> ~*How to Discipline the Flesh*, Kenneth Copeland

*"Restrain thoughts (what we think) produces restrained words (what we say) resulting in restrained actions (what we do)."*
~Rodney Boyd

*"Do not love the world nor the things in the world. If anyone loves the world, the love of the Father is not in him. For all that I in the world, the lust of the flesh, the lust of the eyes and the boastful pride of life, is not from the Father, but is from the world."*
~I John 2:16

There is nothing new under the sun including lust. The d-evil utilized lust in the Garden with Adam and Eve (successfully), tried it in the wilderness with Jesus (unsuccessfully), and continues in the world with you and me (to be determined).

The d-evil still attempts to tempt us (pull us away from who we are in Christ and our purpose and destiny. Hopefully, this book helps by giving us the principles to deal with the principalities. (Ephesians 6:10-19)

In the English language we have one word for love that covers many options. For example, I love hot dogs, I love my dog, I love my wife (Brenda), not necessarily in that order. But in the Greek language there are multiple words for the word, love.

- Eros, or sexual passion/sensual: This is primarily sexual love but not necessarily all there is. I believe that the love for hot dogs is Eros love, a sensual love. When Eros is defiled, it becomes lust.
- Philia, or deep friendship: This is a brotherly love between fellow human beings. There is a city based on this type of love, Philadelphia, the city of brotherly love.
- Ludus, or playful love: This love between friends is having fun between one another, where we kid around, joking, and having fun.
- Agape, or love for everyone: This is known as "the God kind of love" that God has for the world, "For God so *agape* the world that He gave His only begotten Son that whosoever believes in Him should not perish but have everlasting life."

(John 3:16) This love is also the love that we should have for one another. All of the other loves are good if they are governed by Agape Love. When they are not governed by Agape, love turns into lust.
- Pragma, or longstanding love: This type of love is not the type of love that you can fall in or fall out of.
- Philautia, or love of the self: The love of yourself is a good thing but if the love of yourself is more than your love of God, then it has turned into lust.

The Lord's love for us is always there in the midst of trials, troubles, tribulations, and suffering, especially if these things are of our own making. Jeremiah, the weeping (lamenting) prophet speaks of his memory. His lament includes being a man who has seen affliction, been under the rod of His wrath, and made to walk in darkness, (see Lamentations 3:1-18 for a full list of his troubles).

Jeremiah had lost hope. He pleads for the Lord to "Remember my affliction and my wandering, the wormwood and bitterness." (Lamentations 3:19) His soul (mind, will and emotions and the totality of who he was) remembered and is "bowed down within me" (Lamentations 3:20). Jeremiah remembered and recalled to his mind. (Lamentations 3:21) The cause and effect is "I have hope" (that had perished). (Lamentations 3:18, 21)

I believe this passage is necessary for us if we want to live the maximized, overcoming, more than conqueror, victorious, abundant, blessed, successful and prosperous lifestyle.
- The Lord's loving kindnesses' (plureal) indeed never ceases: I thank the Lord that when I sin, when I stop trusting Him that He does not stop loving me and stops being kind to me.
- For His compassions never fail: His love is passionate about loving me and He shows and demonstrates His compassion for me and you.
- They (lovingkindness' and compassion/mercy) never, ever fails me: Human beings will, governmental leaders will, my friends will, my family will, and yes even I will fail myself but God will *never* fail.
- They (His lovingkindness' and compassion/mercy) are new

every morning: When I wake up, I wake up with His lovingkindness and compassion, they are fresh. I can wake up and declare that, "This is the (new) day that the Lord has made, let us rejoice and be glad in it (the day of lovingkindness' and compassion). (Psalm 118:24)

- The Lord is my portion says my soul (that had been rejected from peace, and bent down within, Jeremiah 3:17, 20): Portion= smoothness (of the tongue); also an allotment: - flattery, inheritance, part, X partake, portion.
- Therefore (because of the steadfast love of the Lord) I, Rodney Lewis Boyd, fill in your name) have hope (confident expectation) in Him.
- The Lord is good (not bad) to those who wait (hope) for Him, to the person who seeks Him. It is good that he waits silently for the salvation of the Lord.

NOTE: As I am writing this, it dawned on me that to live the maximized, overcoming, more than a conqueror, victorious, abundant, blessed, successful and prosperous lifestyle, you must do Lamentations 4:25-26

In this book we have been talking about the commandments of God, the Law of God, and the principles of God. Each one is a valuable principle that will change our lives. The final principle is the one that everything else hinges onto.

There was a scribe (among other scribes) who asked Jesus, "What commandment, law, principle is the foremost of all? Jesus did not hesitate in answering him.

*"Jesus answered, the foremost is 'Hear, O Israel! The Lord our God is one Lord.'"*
~the Shema Mark 12:29, Deuteronomy 6:4

*"You believe that God is one. You do well; the demons also believe, and shudder."*
~James 2:19

*Jesus continued, "And you shall love the Lord your God with all*

*your heart, and all your soul and with all your mind and with all your strength. The second is this, you shall love your neighbor as yourself. There is no other commandment, (principle) greater than these."*
~Mark 12:30-31, Leviticus 19:18 addition mine

In the book of James, considered to be one of the first books of the New Testament written, speaks of the Royal Law;

*"If, however you are fulfilling the royal law according to the Scripture, you shall love your neighbor as yourself, you are doing well."*
~James 2:8, Leviticus 19:18

Whatever you do in your life, from business to interpersonal relationships, the practice of Mark 12:30-31 and James 2:19, Leviticus) will give you a maximized, overcoming, more than conqueror, victorious, abundant, blessed, successful, and prosperous life style

# CHAPTER THIRTY TWO

## FINAL THOUGHTS...FINALLY

I have previously written nine books, with this one being number ten. I love the previous books as my written children, but this book, for me, is a significant one. My prayer is that as you have read it, that you are putting the principles into action in your life.

I really believe that it is God's will for you not to be miserable, in poverty, confused, struggling to live your life. As written somewhere in the book, being blessed means to be supremely happy so as to have people envy you as you trust God regardless of what you are going through.

Please check out my website at www.rodneylewisboyd.com.

Be blessed (supremely happy).

Love (Agape') and Holy (because of Him) Kisses (signs of affection)

Rodney

## ABOUT THE AUTHOR

Rodney Boyd is first and foremost a follower of Jesus Christ. He is also a husband, dad and speech-language pathologist. Rodney holds a Master's Degree in Education with emphasis in Speech Communication and has been a practicing Speech-Language Pathologist since 1993. He holds a 2nd degree Black Belt in Wado Ryu Karate; has a passion for music of all styles; and enjoys writing, teaching the Word of God.

Rodney has been married to his high school sweetheart, Brenda, for more than 40 years and together they have one son, Phillip, a daughter-in-law, Jamie, and one granddaughter, Emerson Grace (How Sweet The Sound) Boyd.

Boyd bases his life on Colossians 3:17, "And whatever you do in word or deed, do all in the name of the Lord Jesus, giving thanks through Him to God the Father."

Connect with Rodney on line at:
**www.rodneylewisboyd.com**

## Also by
## Rodney Lewis Boyd

*Never Run a Dead Kata*
*Written that You may Believe*
*Pro-Verb Ponderings*
*Speaking and Hearing the Word of God*
*Chewing the Daily Cud, Vols 1-4*
*On Earth as it is in Heaven*

## Aslo Available from
## WordCrafts Press

**Pondering(s)**
by Wayne Berry

**Donkey Tales**
by Keith Alexis

**I AM**
by Summer McKinney

**What's the Big Idea?**
by Robert G. Lee

www.wordcrafts.net

www.ingramcontent.com/pod-product-compliance
Lightning Source LLC
Chambersburg PA
CBHW072006110526
44592CB00012B/1224